CITYSPOTS
VENICE

Anwer Bati

Written by Anwer Bati
Original photography by Anwer Bati
Front cover photography Gavin Hellier/www.photolibrary.com
Series design based on an original concept by Studio 183 Limited

Produced by Cambridge Publishing Management Limited
Project Editor: Catherine Burch
Layout: Trevor Double
Maps: PC Graphics
Transport map: © Communicarta Limited

Published by Thomas Cook Publishing
A division of Thomas Cook Tour Operations Limited
PO Box 227, Unit 18, Coningsby Road
Peterborough PE3 8SB, United Kingdom
email: books@thomascook.com
www.thomascookpublishing.com
+ 44 (0) 1733 416477
ISBN-13: 978-184157-648-0
ISBN-10: 1-84157-648-4

First edition © 2006 Thomas Cook Publishing
Text © 2006 Thomas Cook Publishing
Maps © 2006 Thomas Cook Publishing
Series Editor/Project Editor: Kelly Anne Pipes
Production/DTP: Steven Collins

Printed and bound in Spain by GraphyCems

CONTENTS

SYMBOLS & ABBREVIATIONS

The following symbols are used throughout this book:

ⓐ address ☏ telephone ⓕ fax ⓔ email ⓦ website address
ⓛ opening times ⓝ public transport connections ⓘ important

The following symbols are used on the maps:

- **ℹ** information office
- **✈** airport
- **✚** hospital
- **Ⓤ** police station
- **▤** bus station
- **▤** railway station
- **Ⓥ** *Vaporetto* stop
- **✝** cathedral
- **❶** numbers denote featured cafés & restaurants

Hotels and restaurants are graded by approximate price as follows:
£ budget **££** mid-range **£££** expensive

▶ *Take a gondola ride through Venice*

Introduction

Venice (Venezia) has almost become a cliché – for art, for romance and for culture. But familiar though it may seem from the paintings, films and vast amount of literature it has inspired, it still has the power to beguile visitors with its beauty and setting. Those who fall under its spell return to marvel again and again, because there is so much to see, with something alluring or intriguing around virtually every corner.

'La Serenissima' ('the most serene') as it was once known, is built on a series of small islands – connected by around 400 foot bridges – in a lagoon at the very north of the Adriatic sea. It is protected from the sea by several other islands and sand bars. It became a major port and trading hub, as well as a great naval power, when it was at its zenith. Its sheer wealth and influence at the time established the city as one of the world's leading cultural centres. As a result, it has lured foreign visitors for centuries, not least British aristocrats undertaking the Grand Tour in the 17th and 18th centuries.

Today, Venice is one of the world's greatest tourist draws, with tourists easily outnumbering locals on most days. In fact, Venice's economy is now mostly geared towards tourism (although it still functions as a port in areas well away from the city centre) and there is no point in pretending that prices are anything but high. Most visitors think that the prices are well worth paying for what can be a magical experience. Quite apart from the consistent beauty of its architecture, and the fact that it is home to some of the world's greatest art treasures, Venice also mounts several cultural events of international importance.

It is a small place, with virtually everything in the city walkable within 30 minutes – wherever you start from. And travelling along the canals is a unique experience, as is arriving by water. Because of its size, Venice is a perfect destination for a long weekend – or even a day trip.

🔺 *View the city from its famous canals*

When to go

SEASONS & CLIMATE

Venice is humid and hot in summer with the odd thunderstorm. Spring and autumn can be wet, but fairly mild, although an easterly wind, the bora, can makes things chillier, particularly in the evening. Because of high tides and winds, there is occasionally mild flooding in some parts of the city (*aqua alta*, or 'high water') between October and April. When flooding occurs, raised wooden walkways are erected around the city to help you to move about. Venice is cold, foggy and damp in winter, but many visitors think that it is then at its most romantic.

COSTS

Venice is an extremely popular destination all year round, but it can get particularly crowded during the main tourist season, from Easter to October. Prices, never low, shoot up then, and you will be lucky to get a hotel room – or any other accommodation – unless you have booked several weeks in advance. The same is true during the Christmas and New Year period, and during Venice's main festivals, particularly *Carnevale* in February. So it's best to go in spring or autumn. That said, November and January are cheaper and noticeably less crowded.

ANNUAL EVENTS

January

Regata delle Befana The first of many regattas during the year, held on Epiphany (6 January). The race takes place along the Grand Canal, with the middle-aged competitors dressed as the good witch Befana.

February
***Carnevale* (Carnival)** On the ten days preceding Ash Wednesday. See pages 12–13 for a full description. Full event details can be obtained from ⓦ www.turismovenezia.it

April
Festa di San Marco The feast day of Venice's patron saint, St Mark (25 April), is celebrated by a gondola race from the island of Sant'Elena to the Punta Della Dogana on the Grand Canal.

May
La Sensa On the Sunday after Ascension Day, the mayor of Venice recreates the 1,000 year-old ceremony in which the doge (or duke) was traditionally rowed to an island to throw a gold ring in to the sea – symbolising Venice's 'marriage' to the sea. Now it is a much less grand affair, and the ceremony takes place off the Lido.

Vogalonga (Held in May or June) A race involving hundreds of boats, in which anyone with access to a rowing vessel can take part. The race (starting at 08.30) sets off from San Marco, heralded by a cannon shot. ⓦ www.vogalonga.it

June
Biennale d'Arte Contemporanea & Architettura Venice's major international contemporary art festival (which takes place from mid-June until the end of October), founded in 1895, takes place every two years in odd-numbered years, such as 2007. There is an architectural festival during even-numbered years. The main venue for the Biennale is the Giardini park in the Castello district, but the festival has now also spread to the Arsenale. There are also several

events in spaces around the city, many of them unofficial. ☎ 041 521 87 11 Ⓦ www.labiennale.org ⏰ 10.00–18.00, Tues–Sun. Admission charge to official exhibitions

June/July
Venezia Suona A Sunday in late June or early July. Rock, folk and jazz festival in venues around the city. Check the website for details, but note that information isn't given very far in advance.
☎ 041 275 00 49 Ⓦ www.veneziasuona.it

July
Festa del Redentore One of Venice's oldest and most important festivals, which takes place the third weekend in July. A pontoon bridge is constructed across the Giudecca canal to the church of Il Redentore, built to celebrate the end of the plague in 1576. An array of boats also gathers, and people picnic on them, as well as enjoying a spectacular firework display at the end of the celebration.

September
Venice film festival (Mostra Internationale D'Arte Cinematografica)
One of the world's most important film festivals (see page 13).

Regata Storica Among Venice's most colourful events, it starts (on the first Sunday in September) with a parade of decorated boats along the Grand Canal, with participants wearing historical costumes. Later there is a series of rowing races, finishing near Ca' Foscari.

October
Venice Marathon Going since 1986, with several changes of route over the years, the marathon (which takes place the last Sunday in

October) starts at Stra, east of Padua, and finishes at the Riva dei Sette Martiri. ☎ 041 532 18 71 ⓦ www.venicemarathon.it

November
Festa della Salute A festival (on 21 November) to give thanks for the end of the plague of 1630, which took 100,000 Venetian lives. A bridge of boats is laid across the Grand Canal to the church of Santa Maria della Salute, and Venetians buy candles to light in the church.

NATIONAL PUBLIC HOLIDAYS
ⓘ Banks and post offices are closed on these days, as are offices. And there is limited public transport on 1 May, Christmas and New Year. Although many shops and restaurants also close in the rest of Italy during public holidays, they tend to stay open in Venice. Note that 21 November is a holiday in Venice only, not the rest of Italy.

New Year's Day 1 Jan
Epiphany 6 Jan
Easter Monday Mar/Apr
Liberation Day and St Mark's Day 25 Apr
Labour Day 1 May
Feast of the Assumption 15 Aug
All Saints' Day 1 Nov
Festa della Salute 21 Nov
Feast of the Immaculate Conception 8 Dec
Christmas Day 25 Dec
Boxing Day (Santo Stefano) 26 Dec

Carnevale & the film festival

Although the word 'carnival' is now used universally, the name literally means 'farewell to meat' – as it is held in the ten days before Lent.

🔵 *Carnival masks make beautiful but pricey souvenirs*

The Carnival started in the 12th century, and once stretched for several months – from Christmas to Lent. It meant the loosening of social rules, not least because the masks and costumes that were worn allowed people of different classes to mix. Balls were organised throughout the city, and both men and women could behave freely, disguised by their masks. As a result, there were many sexual encounters, particularly during the Carnival's most riotous days in the 18th century (when the rake Giacomo Casanova took full advantage).

Carnival came to an end in 1797, when the French, under Napoleon, conquered the city. It was revived by locals in 1979, at first in a small way. But it soon became a major tourist attraction, just as it had been in its heyday. Now, Venice throngs with costumed tourists during Carnival, and hotel rooms have to be booked months in advance.

The other major festival in Venice is the film festival. Officially part of the Biennale, the film festival is the world's oldest and most prestigious, founded in 1932. Two years later a jury was formed to dish out prizes. Then, in 1952, the festival jury inaugurated the famous Golden Lion award.

The festival is attended by many top international film makers and movie stars, and is a showcase for both mainstream and art house films. It takes place on the Lido, in the Palazzo del Cinema and the old Casino – both near the Hotel des Bains and the Excelsior (where many of the stars stay).

In addition to the festival are various unofficial cinema events around Venice. You can get season tickets and tickets for individual films, but it would be sensible to book well in advance.

🄰 Palazzo del Cinema, Lungomare Marconi 90 🛈 041 521 87 11
🆆 www.labienalle.org

History

Venice was founded following invasions of northern Italy by the Lombards and other Germanic tribes starting in the middle of the 6th century. As a result, people from the mainland sought refuge on the islands of the Venetian lagoon.

Although technically under the control of the Byzantine empire, the islanders formed a republic ruled by an elected doge (or duke) in 697. The republic eventually drew away from Byzantine rule, and Venice as we now know it then gradually evolved – both physically and as a nation state – with a ducal palace erected on the site of the present building in the early 9th century.

According to tradition, in around 828, two merchants from Torcello stole the body of St Mark the Evangelist from Alexandria, and Venice subsequently adopted St Mark as its patron saint. His symbol – a winged lion – also became the city's emblem. A shrine built to commemorate the saint would eventually become St Mark's Basilica.

The republic of Venice developed a unique system of government, with doges (who ruled for life) chosen by election. Although superficially democratic, by the end of the 13th century the state was, in reality, controlled by an oligarchy composed of nobles and leading merchants. The doge's own power was constrained by a series of councils and committees.

Venice's contacts with the Byzantine empire, as well as its growing emergence as a naval power – after the defeats of several enemies and rivals – meant it began to emerge as a military and trading force to be reckoned with. With its links in the east, the Crusades – during which the city made money out of transporting crusaders – were a crucial factor in Venice's growth as a major power and commercial centre dominating the Adriatic. The

Venetians were already known for their arrogance and aggression abroad, and they were foremost in the sacking and pillage of Constantinople in 1204, coming back with huge amounts of booty.

By the 13th century, Venice had effectively acquired a trading empire in the region, established through a string of ports it controlled. Venice also acquired territory on the Italian mainland, so that by the beginning of the 15th century the Venetian empire was at its zenith and became the leading power in the eastern Mediterranean – and the most substantial naval force in Christendom.

Venice continued to prosper economically and artistically during the 16th century, producing great painters as well as composers and architects. But conflicts, particularly with the Ottoman empire in the 15th and 16th centuries, slowly led to the empire's decline.

Venice was no longer a significant power by the 18th century, and in 1797 Napoleon Bonaparte's soldiers invaded it, deposing the last doge, Ludovico Manin. Napoleon ceded control of the city, and its remaining territories to Hapsburg Austria, but the French took over again from 1806 until 1814 – when Venice became Austrian again – and continued to stagnate. It finally became part of the newly united kingdom of Italy in 1866.

Although the port at Marghera and the industrial area at Mestre (both on the mainland) were developed in the early 20th century, Venice's main raison d'etre became tourism, not least after a railway link to the mainland was built in 1846. A road bridge was added in 1932. Both these developments faced strong local opposition from traditionalists. Over the last 50 years or so the fabric of the city has suffered from industrial pollution, flooding (an age-old problem, but particularly severe in 1966), and the fact that the city was sinking – though this has been slowed down thanks to measures taken over the last few decades. Venice was declared a World Heritage Site by UNESCO in 1987.

Lifestyle

In a way, it is difficult to talk about the Venetian lifestyle, because most visitors, particularly in the main tourist season, will hardly see it. In fact, all you will see are the people who serve you in shops, restaurants and cafés – plus, of course, some of the estimated 13 to 14 million other visitors who go there each year.

The population of the city has declined rapidly during the 20th century, and now stands at around 65,000. In the summer high season, local residents are often outnumbered by tourists, especially as many Venetians not working in the tourist industry flee the city in August.

To get a taste of the 'real' Venice, you will have to visit some of the outlying and somewhat rundown areas off the main tourist track – such as Cannaregio and Castello. Alternatively, get up early in the morning and see Venetians going about their business or having a coffee before the daily influx of tourists. But although much of native Venetian life is behind closed doors to tourists (apart from, perhaps, in winter), the one thing that all Venetians share – whether they are aristocrats or local artisans – is a huge pride in their city and its history. And they expect visitors to respect the place.

Venice has always attracted many wealthy and glamorous visitors. So the locals, smart and pretty refined themselves, expect tourists to show a reasonable level of decorum in both their behaviour and dress – particularly in churches. You are also expected to put your litter in a bin, for instance.

Despite the money tourists bring in, you can be forgiven for feeling that visitors are more tolerated than loved. So, although many people are helpful and friendly, don't expect a particularly warm welcome everywhere you go. You should also be prepared for high prices for virtually everything – particularly near the main tourist attractions. There is often dual pricing: tourists pay much more than Venetians even on the water buses, for instance.

On the plus side, many Venetians, over half of whom work in the tourist industry, speak English. Venetians also have their own vocabulary in addition to regular Italian: 'campo', for instance is a small square and any road called 'Fondamenta' runs along a canal.

⏶ *Venice's covered market on the Rialto – a taste of local life*

Culture

Venice has been synonymous with great art, wonderful architecture and sublime music since as far back as the 14th century. But it was really the 16th and 17th centuries, even though the city's economic fortunes were in serious decline by then, that saw the greatest flourishing of art and culture. And Venice's wealth ensured that its churches and buildings – both public and private – were lavishly decorated. Commerce and culture have always gone hand in hand in Venice, and in many ways still do.

Most of the grander buildings were built to be seen from the canals, from which they would have been approached. Styles range from Byzantine-influenced palaces dating from as early as the 13th century, with their characteristic simple rounded arches, to the more elaborate pointed arches (the style called ogee) and tracery of the Gothic 14th- and 15th-century buildings – including Ca' d'Oro and the Doge's Palace. Then there are sandstone Renaissance buildings with classical columns, and the even more elaborate and heavily ornamented Baroque buildings of the 17th century, such as Ca' Pesaro. Venice is constantly undergoing renovation, so don't be surprised if you encounter this at museums and churches during your visit.

Venice's many churches, each in their own small square (or *campo*) have the same range of styles, and some of them contain works of art which would grace any major museum. There is little modern architecture in Venice, though several contemporary interiors.

Venetian painters often painted Venice and its richer inhabitants, even though the subjects may have been ostensibly biblical or classical. And they reflected the wealth and finery of its citizens.

The first notable Venetian painter was the 14th-century artist Paolo Veneziano – influenced by Byzantine art, as were his contemporaries. But it was the brothers Giovanni and Gentile Bellini, in the following century, who became internationally famous for their vividly coloured works. Many of Gentile Bellini's works can be found in the Correr Museum.

The Bellinis used egg-based tempera paint, but the greatest Venetian masters – from the 16th century onwards – including Titian, Veronese, Giorgione and Tintoretto, used oil, and fully exploited the medium's ability to enable the subtle use of light, shade, atmosphere and texture. Some of their finest and best-known works can be found in the Accademia gallery.

The 18th century saw the last flowering of Venetian art, with painters such as Giambattista Tiepolo, and his son Giandomenico. And, of course, Canaletto, whose numerous images of Venice – many of them in Britain, bought by aristocrats on the Grand Tour – are familiar to those who have never been anywhere near the place.

La Fenice opera house hosts opera, drama and ballet

If it's modern art that interests you, then outside the years of the art Biennale, the place to go is the Guggenheim Museum, which is conveniently near the Accademia – although there are several small private galleries displaying work of varying quality around the city, and there are many high quality modern works at Ca' Pesaro. The Palazzo Grassi is now also a leading modern art museum.

Apart from the Biennale, Venice's other great modern event is the film festival. However, Venice only has two regular cinemas: the Giorgione Movie, in Cannaregio, and the Multisala Astra, on the Lido.

Classical music is well served in Venice and there are concerts throughout the year in locations (including churches) around the city. For detailed listings visit ⓦ www.turismovenezia.it

As for the performing arts, you will be able to find theatre at the beautiful Teatro Goldoni (classic Italian plays); opera, dance and ballet at the La Fenice opera house and the Teatro Malibran; and contemporary dance at the Teatro Fondamenta Nuove.

ENTRANCE TICKETS

There are several types of multi-entrance tickets available from the museums, the tourist office and the offices of the ACTV-Vela organisation at Piazalle Roma, and near San Marco (ⓒ 041 2424 ⓒ 08.00–20.00). You can also get a Venice card, which entitles you to enter city museums and use other facilities. Check with ⓦ www.venicecard.com.

A multi-entry ticket to Venice's main churches is available from any of the churches which charge for entry.

❚ *The river offers intimate glimpses of Venice*

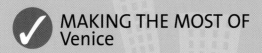

MAKING THE MOST OF
Venice

Shopping

WHERE TO SHOP

The main shopping area, particularly for fashion, is around Mercerie, just off San Marco. Some of the biggest designer names are located in the area between San Marco and La Fenice opera house, particularly in Calle Larga XXII Marzo. Venice also has many less well-known fashion and shoe shops (Italian shoes and leather are particularly good) to at least have a look at.

Some of the better shops selling local crafts are in or around Campo Santo Stefano, Calle della Mandola, and the Dorsoduro district. The finest glass, which Venice is famous for – often ornate and highly decorated – comes from the nearby island of Murano (see page 132) The best lace is from the island of Burano (see page 135).

The skill of making marbled paper was lost in Venice in the 19th century, until it was revived in the 1970s. There are several styles of beautiful paper as well as notebooks and other stationery.

Most of the better antique shops are clustered around Campo San Maurizio, just five minutes from San Marco, and La Fenice.

SHOPPING TIPS

❶ You are unlikely to find any bargains in Venice, so attuned is it to tourists. There are plenty of tacky tourist and souvenir shops and street hawkers selling fake designer goods. But Venice also has genuine local specialities – such as lace, marbled paper, glass and carnival masks – made by skilled artisans. However, be aware that some shops sell inferior versions of these products (quite often imported) in the main tourist areas.

Other items to look out for are the rich local fabrics, jewellery, metalwork and old prints.

The most colourful food market is held near the Rialto Bridge (🕒 07.30–13.00 Mon–Sat). The Rialto (the San Polo side of the bridge) is also the scene of a daily market selling clothes, trinkets, leather goods and souvenirs. There is a quieter food market in Via Garibaldi in the Castello district (Mon–Sat), and a regular market in Rio Terra San Leonardo in Cannaregio.

USEFUL SHOPPING PHRASES

What time do the shops open/close?
A che ora aprono/chiudono i negozi?
Ah keh awra ahprawnaw/kewdawnaw ee nehgotsee?

How much is this?
Quant' è?
Kwahnteh?

Can I try this on?
Posso provarlo?
Pawssaw prawvarrlaw?

My size is ...
La mia taglia è ...
Lah meeyah tahlyah eh ...

I'll take this one, thank you.
Prenderò questo, grazie.
Prehndehroh kwestaw, grahtsyeh.

Can you show me the one in the window/this one?
Può mostrarmi quello in vetrina/questo?
Pooh oh mawstrahrmee kwehllaw een vehtreenah/kwehstaw?

This is too large/too small/too expensive.
Questo è troppo grande/troppo piccolo/troppo caro.
*Kwestaw eh tropaw grahndeh/tropaw peekawlaw/
trawpaw kahraw.*

Eating & drinking

Even the most fervent fan of Venice won't claim that you will always get a great meal in the city. Since so many restaurants are geared towards tourists, it is very difficult to get a cheap and cheerful meal anywhere near the centre. But you will do better in outlying areas such as Cannaregio, Castello, San Polo and Santa Croce.

As a general rule, the nearer you are to San Marco, the more expensive a place will be. Prices, even for a glass of wine, can be high.

Unusually, some of the best food served in Venice is to be found in the more upmarket hotels, and the prices are sometimes more reasonable for what you actually get than in less smart eateries. Hotel restaurants also stay open on Sunday and Monday evenings, when many other places are closed.

There is a good range of different types of eating and drinking places in Venice. They range from ordinary bars and cafés to *bacari* (wine bars, a recently revived tradition, which serve tapas-style snacks called *cichetti*), more sophisticated *enoteca* (also wine bars, with more elaborate food), simple trattorias and *osterias*, plus the more formal restaurants. You will also find pizzerias, ice cream parlours (*gelateria*), tea shops, bakeries, and cake and pastry shops.

THINGS TO CHECK

Some restaurants and bars are closed out of season, so you should check in advance and it is always advisable to book at popular restaurants.

Bills normally include service (and almost always a cover charge). If not, you should pay up to 10% for service.

Many small cafés and bars sell mini-pizzas, sandwiches in buns, *panini* (toasted sandwiches), *tremezzini* (regular sandwiches) and other food to take out. But picnicking is frowned on in Venice, particularly in and near San Marco (you will see signs warning you of fines). What's more, there are few benches to sit on in the city. But you might try Zattere – along the side of the Giudecca canal – not far from the Accademia gallery.

THE BIG SMOKE

Although a large proportion of Italians smoke, Italy now has some of the strictest anti-smoking laws in Europe. Essentially you can't smoke in public buildings or enclosed spaces such as restaurants and bars. But you can still light up at outside tables.

◆ *Enjoy a meal with a view*

Venetian cuisine isn't the best you will find in Italy, but there are many excellent local specialities, and fish and seafood are always a good choice. These specialities include: *acciuge* (anchovies), *anguilla* (eel), *baccala* (a salt cod dip), *boveleti* (small snails), *carpaccio* (raw, lean, thinly sliced fillet of beef), *cozze* (mussels), *fegato alla veneziana* (calves' liver and onions), *folpi* (baby octopus), *frito misto di mare* (fried seafood) *granchio* (crab), *granseola* (spider crab), *polenta* (cornmeal cake, usually firm and grilled, sometimes less

USEFUL DINING PHRASES

I would like a table for ... people.
Vorrei un tavolo per ... persone.
Vawrray oon tahvawlaw perr ... perrsawneh.

Waiter/waitress!
Cameriere/cameriera!
Cahmehryereh/cahmehryera!

May I have the bill, please?
Mi dà il conto, per favore?
Mee dah eel cawntaw, perr fahvawreh?

Could I have it well-cooked/medium/rare please?
Potrei averlo ben cotto/mediamente cotto/poco cotto, per favore?
Pawtray ahvehrlaw behn cawtaw/mehdeeyahmehnteh cawtaw/pawcaw cawtaw perr fahvawreh?

I am a vegetarian. Does this contain meat?
Sono vegetariano/vegetariana (fem.). Contiene carne?
Sawnaw vejetahreeahnaw/vejetahreeahnah.
Contyehneh kahrneh?

> ## RESTAURANT CATEGORIES
> The approximate price bands into which restaurants fall are
> based on the average cost of a three-course evening meal for
> one person, excluding drinks. Remember, though, that lunch or
> a set menu will often be cheaper.
> £ Up to €30   ££ €30–70   £££ Above €70

solid), *prosciutto San Daniele* (the best local ham), *risi e bisi* (rice and
peas, sometimes with ham or bacon), *risotto di mare* (risotto – rice
cooked in butter and stock – with seafood), *risotto in nero* (risotto
with cuttlefish or squid ink; pasta is also served this way), *sarde in
soar* (sardines marinated with onions, pine nuts, raisins and
vinegar), *seppie* (cuttlefish), *spaghetti alle vongole* (spaghetti with
clams in a white wine sauce) and *tripa* (tripe, usually with onions).

Many of the wines of the Veneto region (the hinterland behind
Venice) are well known internationally, and improving all the time.
Its sensible to drink local wine, as the prices will be lower. Look out
for Valpolicella (a full-bodied red, which can be drunk chilled),
Bardolino (another robust red, good with meat), Soave (a smooth
white), Raboso (a warming, tannic red) and Valadige (red, white or
rosé). Try to go for the *superiore* or *classico* labels of these wines. The
region's famous light sparkling wine, Prosecco, is normally drunk as
an aperitif.

The local spirit is grappa (a marc brandy made from grapes),
and the liqueur of choice is Amaretto, which has an almond and
apricot flavour.

The region also produces several good dessert wines. A favourite
Venetian tipple (as an aperitif) is Spritz – consisting of white wine,
Campari and soda or fizzy water.

Entertainment & nightlife

Venice can turn into something of a ghost town at night, particularly outside the main tourist season, but a lot of people like it that way. Many bars and cafés close by 22.00 (or even earlier), though there are some that are open until 23.00 or 24.00. Restaurants rarely serve after 22.30 or 23.00, but you might be able to get a late-night snack in a bar. The more expensive hotels serve drinks and snacks until later.

There are, however, a few places – the number is increasing – that are open late, and some of them have live music, others recorded. Clubs and discos are even more difficult to come by, but there are a couple. Areas to head to for activity after 23.00 include Campo Santa Margherita, Campo Santo Stefano, Campo San Polo, Fondamenta della Misericordia and Campo San Barnaba.

If it's performances you want in the evening, then you're well served in terms of classical concerts, opera, dance and, occasionally, jazz (check listings on Ⓦ www.caligola.it for jazz). But rock and other contemporary music aren't high on Venice's agenda, not least because of stringent local noise laws. That said, there is the odd event.

● *Evening entertainment at a casino*

For major opera and ballet performances, you will have to book well in advance. For listings, get a copy of *Un Ospite di Venezia* – a fortnightly publication, partly in English, free from hotels and tourist offices (ⓦ www.unospitedivenezia.it). It also contains useful transport and other information. If you attend an evening performance, try to eat first, as you may find it difficult to get a meal afterwards.

Things get a bit livelier in the evenings during Venice's major festivals – particularly the Biennale, Venezia Suona and film festival. You can, of course, book to see the films. Otherwise, Venice only has two cinemas, both with two screens. The Giorgione shows the occasional English-language film, but most are dubbed in Italian. The same is true of the Multisala Astra. However, in the summer you can watch movies in the open air every evening in Campo San Polo. Entries to the film festival (usually in their original language) are shown there during the run of the festival. You can book tickets for most events through ACTV- Vela. ⓐ Santa Croce 509, Piazzale Roma ⓛ 08.30–18.30 daily ⓐ San Marco 1810, Calle dei Fuseri ⓛ 08.30–18.30 Mon–Sat. Call centre ⓣ 041 2424

Most water buses stop running before midnight, though there are some night services (check on ⓦ www.actv.it) and you will still be able to get water taxis – although these aren't cheap.

ROMANTIC VENICE
Many Venetians take a stroll after dinner to stop off somewhere for coffee or an ice cream; indeed, walking around Venice at night, particularly when it's warmer, is one of the romantic attractions of the place. Taking a gondola, water bus or taxi along the Grand Canal is another night-time pleasure.

Sport & relaxation

There are very few opportunities for sport in Venice, unless you want to participate in regattas such as Vogalonga (see page 9), or indeed the Venice marathon (see page 10). If you want, you can learn to row. For lessons try Reale Societa Canottieri Bucintoro, a rowing club that began in 1882 (ⓐ Zattere, Dorsoduro 15 ⓣ 041 522 20 55 ⓦ www.bucintoro.org).

The only hotel in Venice itself with a swimming pool is the luxurious Cipriani on Giudecca. Otherwise, there is a public pool in the Cannaregio area: Piscina Comunale Di Sant'Alvise (ⓐ Calle del Capitello, Campo Sant'Alvise ⓛ check opening times with tourist office).

There are a handful of gyms in Venice, including Palestra International Club near the Rialto (ⓐ Sotoportego dei Amai ⓣ 041 528 98 30) and Eutonia Club (ⓐ Calle Renier, Dorsoduro ⓣ 041 522 86 18 ⓦ www.eutonia.net).

If you go to the Lido, however, there are several more sporting options. These include cycling. Bruno Lazzari (ⓐ Gran Viale 21B ⓣ 041 526 80 19) and Giorgio Barberi (ⓐ Gran Viale 79A ⓣ 041 526 14 90) are two places to rent bikes, but there are also others.

The Lido also has beaches and a golf club, Circolo Golf Venezia (ⓐ Strada Vecchia 1 ⓣ 041 731 333 ⓦ www.circologolfvenezia.it). You can play tennis and rent rackets at Tennis Club Ca' del Moro (ⓐ Via Ferruccio Parri 6 ⓣ 041 770 965). Additionally, the club has a gym, a pool and other sporting facilities.

Essentially, walking is your main fitness option in Venice itself – and you will do plenty of that.

SPECTATOR SPORTS

Other than watching the city's regattas, or the marathon, the only spectator sport in Venice is football. The AC Venezia ground is in the east of the city at Sant'Elena, beyond the Castello district. The club once reached Italy's Serie A league (in 1999), but mostly languishes in the 2nd and 3rd divisions. Games take place on Saturdays and Sundays (June–Sept). Check the website for fixtures

ⓦ www.veneziacalcio.it

🔺 *Relaxing in a gondola*

Accommodation

Venice boasts more than 200 hotels of all types, and even more B&Bs and apartments. Even some of the cheaper hotels are on canals or housed in lovely old buildings. What's more, there are plenty of upmarket hotels if you want to splash out on a romantic weekend.

Many hotels include a continental or buffet breakfast in their rates; others charge a hefty supplement. Tour operators offer some of the best deals, as do internet sites where you combine your flight with a hotel, but book well in advance. You are likely to get good deals in spring, autumn and winter, and during the week.

❶ As a general rule, the nearer a hotel is to San Marco or the Grand Canal, the more expensive it will be.

The Venice tourist website (ⓦ www.turismovenezia.it) carries a comprehensive list of hotels, their facilities and locations, and of self-catering apartments for rent in case you want to stay for more than a few days.

PRICE RATING

The ratings indicate average price per double room per night. Some rooms, particularly those overlooking canals, may be more or less expensive than the ratings suggested. But staying in Venice is expensive, even for the simplest hotels.

£ Up to €150   ££ €150–250   £££ above €250

HOTELS

Locanda Ca' Foscari £ You'll get a warm welcome in this comfortable, family-run hotel. Not all the rooms have bathrooms. ⓐ Dorsoduro 3887 B, Calle della Frescada ☎ 041 71 04 01
🔃 www.locandacafoscari.com

Locanda Salieri £ Ten rooms in this straightforward hotel, six with bathrooms. Located near the station and the Piazzale Roma. ⓐ Santa Croce 160, Fondamdenta Minotto ☎ 041 71 00 35
🔃 www.hotelsalieri.com

Agli Alboretti £–££ Popular place, with a good restaurant and pleasant rooms. Near the Accademia. ⓐ Dorsoduro 882, Rio Tera Foscarini ☎ 041 523 00 58 🔃 www.aglialboretti.com

Falier £–££ Smallish but well-kept rooms and reasonable prices. Not far from the station. ⓐ Santa Croce 130, Salizada San Pantalon ☎ 041 71 08 82 🔃 www.hotelfalier.com

Locanda del Ghetto £–££ A small, modest hotel with pleasant rooms. ⓐ Cannaregio 2892, Campo del Ghetto Nouvo ☎ 041 275 92 92 🔃 www.locandadelghetto.net

Ca' Pisani ££ In an old merchant's house near the Accademia, this is a hotel with contemporary interior décor. ⓐ Dorsoduro 979 A ☎ 041 240 14 11 🔃 www.capisanihotel.it or www.designhotels.com

Ca' Vendramin di Santa Fosca ££ An appealing small new hotel in an old palazzo on a quiet canal in the Cannaregio area. ⓐ Cannaregio 2400 ☎ 041 275 01 25 🔃 www.hotelcavendramin.com

DD 724 ££ A small (seven rooms), very modern hotel near the Guggenheim Museum. ⓐ Dorsoduro 724 ❶ 041 277 02 62 Ⓦ www.dd724.it

Liassidi Palace ££–£££ A very comfortable, stylish, well-appointed modernised 14th-century palazzo in a good location, on a canal. A member of Small Luxury Hotels of the World ⓐ Castello, Ponte dei Greci 3405 ❶ 041 520 56 58 Ⓦ www.slh.com/liassidi

Cipriani £££ More a resort than a hotel and, located on the island of Giudecca, the only hotel in Venice with a pool (plus any number of other facilities, including three very good restaurants and beautiful rooms). The swishest address in town – but at a price. ⓐ Giudecca 10 ❶ 041 520 77 45 Ⓦ www.hotelcipriani.com

Danieli £££ One of Venice's most famous hotels in the former home of a doge. With a grand reception area and magnificent decorations. Also has a roof terrace. ⓐ Castello 4196, Riva degli Schiavoni ❶ 041 522 64 80 Ⓦ www.starwood.com

Gritti Palace £££ Legendary hotel decorated with priceless antiques: opulent but intimate. On the Grand Canal. ⓐ Campo Santa Maria del Giglio 2467 ❶ 041 79 46 11 Ⓦ www.starwoodhotels.com

Westin Europa & Regina £££ Somewhat cheaper than some of the other leading hotels in Venice. Luxurious, with excellent service. Superb location on the Grand Canal opposite Santa Maria della Salute. Also has one of the best restaurants in town. Several rooms

◀ *The sumptuous Gritti Palace overlooks the water*

have a canal view. ❷ San Marco 2159 ❶ 041 240 00 01
Ⓦ www.westin.com

B&BS

Venice has many bed and breakfast establishments, some of them
very stylish indeed, others more modest. Prices range from around
€40 per night for a double room to more than €200. Among the
most stylish are those listed below.

Ca' Della Corte ££ A stylishly decorated 16th-century house with a
courtyard. The rooms are bright and spacious. ❷ Dorsoduro 3560,
Corte Surian ❶ 041 71 58 77 Ⓦ www.cadellacorte.com

Palazzo Malcanton ££ Owned by Englishman Nick Blair-Fish, this is a
lavishly restored 15th-century house with a garden next to a canal.
Near the station and Piazzale Roma. ❷ Santa Croce 49, Salizada San
Pantalon ❶ 041 71 09 31 Ⓦ www.venice4you.co.uk

YOUTH HOSTELS

Venice has a number of youth hostels of varying degrees of comfort
and cleanliness. They all charge around €25–€50 per room per night.

Casa Santa Dorotea ❷ Cannaregio 2927 ❶ 041 71 70 22
Ostello Venezia ❷ Fondamenta delle Zitelle 86 ❶ 041 523 82 11
Ⓦ www.ostellionline.org

Residenza Universitaria San Toma ❷ San Polo 2846 ❶ 041 275 09 30
Ⓦ www.esuvenezia.it

---

❶ *Classic Venetian style at Westin Europa & Regina*

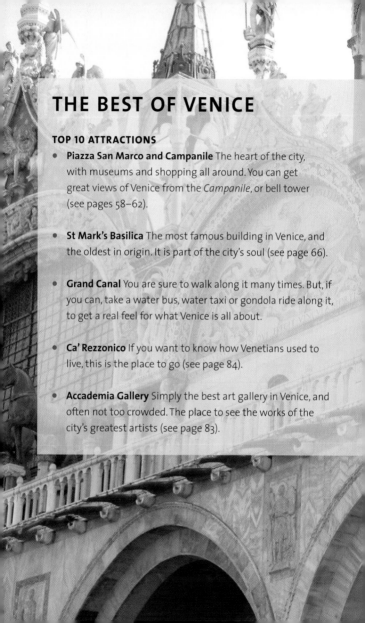

THE BEST OF VENICE

TOP 10 ATTRACTIONS

- **Piazza San Marco and Campanile** The heart of the city, with museums and shopping all around. You can get great views of Venice from the *Campanile*, or bell tower (see pages 58–62).

- **St Mark's Basilica** The most famous building in Venice, and the oldest in origin. It is part of the city's soul (see page 66).

- **Grand Canal** You are sure to walk along it many times. But, if you can, take a water bus, water taxi or gondola ride along it, to get a real feel for what Venice is all about.

- **Ca' Rezzonico** If you want to know how Venetians used to live, this is the place to go (see page 84).

- **Accademia Gallery** Simply the best art gallery in Venice, and often not too crowded. The place to see the works of the city's greatest artists (see page 83).

- **Rialto Bridge** One of the focal points of the city. It buzzes during the market (see page 60).

- **Boat trip into town** If you can afford a water taxi (not cheap), or take a water bus from the airport, Lido or islands, this is the way to approach Venice. One of the great experiences, which will take you back in history (see page 52).

- **Santa Maria Gloriosa dei Frari** Perhaps the most important church in Venice – with works by Titian and Giovanni Bellini (see page 96).

- **Guggenheim Museum** Highly popular, but surprisingly peaceful. It's on the Grand Canal and houses Venice's best collection of modern art (see page 85).

- **Ca' d'Oro** This 15th-century merchant's palazzo has one of Venice's finest façades, and an impressive collection of paintings (see page 110).

◗ *The magnificence of St Mark's Basilica*

Your brief guide to seeing and experiencing the best of Venice, depending on the time you have available.

HALF-DAY: VENICE IN A HURRY

If you are only in Venice for a short time, then you should head to San Marco and the area immediately around it, as so many of the city's main sites and shopping areas are only a couple of minutes away. Have a drink or a coffee in Florian or Quadri, go to the top of the Campanile, and admire St Mark's Basilica. Then you can decide whether to shop, go to the Correr Museum for art, or look at the inside of the Doge's Palace. Alternatively, take a water bus (*vaporetto*), water taxi or gondola down the Grand Canal.

1 DAY: TIME TO SEE A LITTLE MORE

If you have a full day in Venice, then – in addition to the above – you shouldn't miss the Accademia gallery, to see the greatest glories of Venetian art. Ca' Rezzonica, nearby, is worth visiting to get an idea of Venetian interiors when the city was still wallowing in wealth. And you should definitely go to the Rialto Bridge – particularly in the morning when the lively food market takes place.

2–3 DAYS: SHORT CITY BREAK

If you are going to be in Venice for a long weekend, then head for the Dorsoduro, Santa Croce and San Polo areas. In Dorsoduro, you will find the famous Guggenheim collection and the nearby church of Santa Maria della Salute, one of the city's main landmarks. Not far away in the districts of Santa Croce and San Polo are the magnificent church of Santa Maria Glorioso dei Frari and the Scuola Grande di San Rocco. If you want to relax, go to one of the cafés or pizzerias along Zattere and get a view of Giudecca. And – if you can afford it – pop into Harry's Bar or the Gritti Palace hotel for a drink.

LONGER: ENJOYING VENICE TO THE FULL

If you're staying longer, you can explore some of the quieter outlying areas. To get away from the bustle, head to Cannaregio for the lovely church of Madonna dell'Orto. If you are interested in ships and naval history, the collection at the Museo Storico Navale in the Arsenale area might well excite you. You should also have time to take a trip to the island of Giudecca, where you will have fine views of Venice, and maybe get a drink at the famous Cipriani hotel. For a change in atmosphere, and some time on the beach, go to the Lido. Alternatively, head out to the charming small islands of Torcello, Murano and Burano.

⬤ *Santa Maria della Salute is a useful, beautiful landmark*

Something for nothing

The cheapest thing in Venice is also one of the most enjoyable: simply walking around and being seduced by the beauty of the city. The Grand Canal is hard to beat. Sunset is also something to behold. There will be something stunning or fascinating virtually everywhere you go. In fact, you need never enter a museum. And window shopping in Venice's designer, antique and craft shops costs nothing.

Venice also has many small squares (*campi*) with their own churches, where you can toy with a cup of coffee or glass of wine for as long as you like, and watch everyone else going by. You might also see street entertainers and buskers from time to time, particularly in summer. Many of them will ask you for money, but you aren't obliged to pay.

Several of Venice's churches charge tourists for entry, but the charges are modest, and inside you will often find great works of art – in the places for which they were intended – which most major museums around the world would kill for. You will also be able to hear free music performances in some churches.

The many colourful regattas staged in Venice, and events like the marathon, are also free to watch, and you can easily get caught up in the festive atmosphere, as you will if you are in town for the free Venezia Suona music festival (rock, reggae, jazz and more).

There are few green spaces in Venice, although there are gardens at the southern end of the Castello district, including the Giardini where the Biennale takes place.

▶ *The magic of sunset*

When it rains

It can rain at any time of the year in Venice, with sometimes dramatic thunderstorms in the summer. So you should go prepared.

❶ Check out one of the many weather websites such as ⓦ www.weather.com or ⓦ www.bbc.co.uk/weather before you leave.

That said, rain shouldn't stop you sitting under a bar or café umbrella in one of the *campi*, or retreating inside. If you go to Florian, the interior and atmosphere there is well worth the visit. You could equally well have a drink at one of the grander hotels, or Harry's Bar – which, though expensive, needn't cost you much more than a drink in San Marco.

Of course, the rain will give you the perfect opportunity to visit the churches and museums you previously walked by. Or you can go back to one you whizzed round, and take a more considered look at the exhibits. And a *vaporetto* or water taxi ride along one of the canals can still be rewarding, as you can sit under cover.

Some people actually enjoy walking in the Venetian rain: the views are the same, but not so great for photographs. The Rialto market will be just as buzzy, and there is nothing to stop you stepping into the main designer shops.

You could also head to a cinema, if you speak Italian. In any case, the rain will probably not last that long, and in the summer, the streets will dry very quickly.

▶ *Ca' d'Oro: the best known palazzo on the Grand Canal*

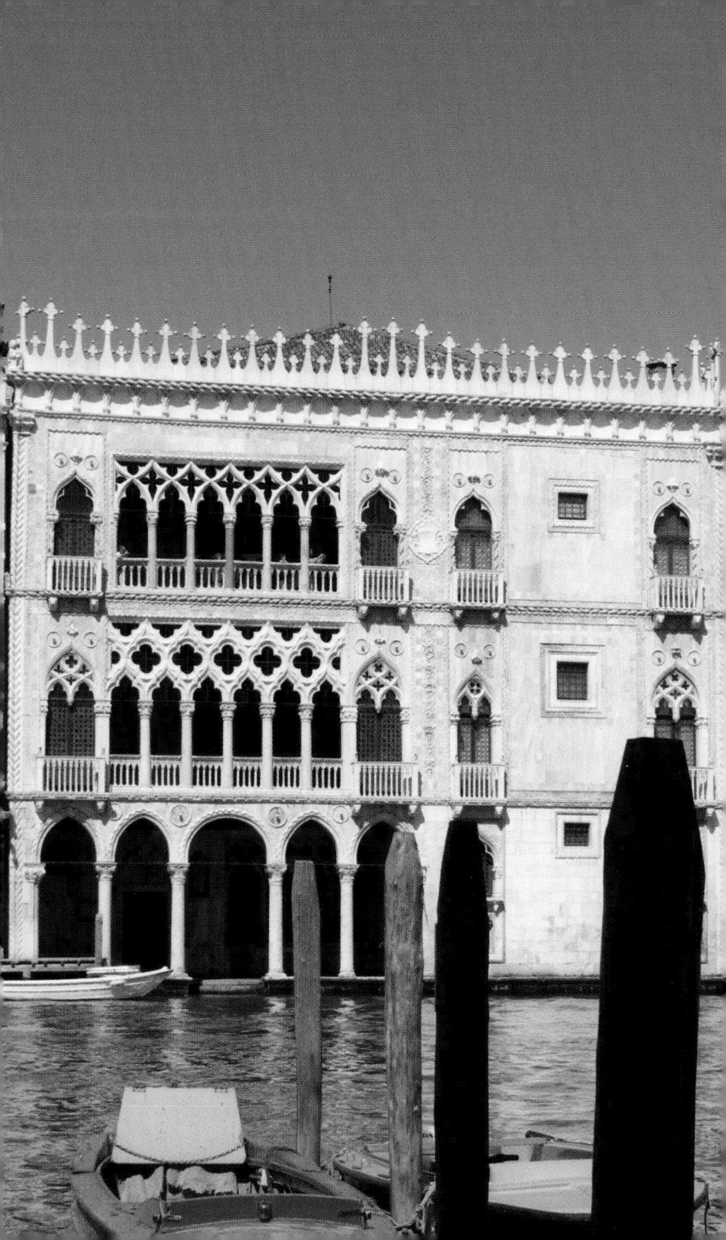

On arrival

TIME DIFFERENCES

Italian clocks follow Central European Time (CET). During Daylight Saving Time (end Mar–end Oct), the clocks are put forward one hour. In the Italian summer, at noon, time elsewhere is as follows:

Australia Eastern Standard Time 20.00, Central Standard Time 19.30, Western Standard Time 18.00
New Zealand 22.00
South Africa 12.00
UK and Republic of Ireland 11.00
USA and Canada Newfoundland Time 07.30, Atlantic Canada Time 07.00, Eastern Time 06.00, Central Time 05.00, Mountain Time 04.00, Pacific Time 03.00, Alaska 02.00

ARRIVING
By air

The main airport serving Venice is Marco Polo, at Tessera, on the mainland around 8 km (5 miles) from the city. Arrivals are on the ground floor. You will find ATMs, currency exchanges (*cambio*), and information and hotel booking desks, as well as shops and a bar.
❶ 041 260 92 60 **ⓦ** www.veniceairport.it

You can either get into Venice from Marco Polo airport by land or by water. If you go by land, you have the choice of taking a taxi to Piazzale Roma (around 20 minutes). If you want to pay by credit card, book the taxi in the arrivals hall. Alternatively, you can take an ATVO coach, and buy your ticket from the office near the baggage reclaim area. The service runs every 30 minutes or so. Or you could take an ACTV city bus (a somewhat longer journey, and you have to purchase a separate ticket for each suitcase you have). Again, buy tickets from near the baggage reclaim area. Validate your ticket on board, by putting it in the machine on the bus.

🔺 Water buses are a good way to get around

Buses stop at the Piazzale Roma in Venice, so you will then have to take a *vaporetto* (water bus) or water taxi from there to your accommodation, unless it is in walking distance.

For *vaporetto* timetables and routes, check Ⓦ www.actv.it

If you opt for getting into Venice by water – a far more enjoyable but more expensive option – you have two choices. You can take a ferry run by the Societa Alilaguna (Ⓣ 041 523 57 75 Ⓦ www.alilaguna.com), which has three routes, each of which runs hourly. The Blu route goes via Murano and the Lido to San Zaccharia and San Marco. The Rosso route also goes via Murano and the Lido, and then to Arsenale, San Marco and Zattere. Both take about one hour. The Oro route goes directly to San Marco and is faster, but more expensive. You can buy tickets in the arrivals hall or on board. To walk to the landing stage (left outside the terminal), allow ten minutes.

Otherwise you can take a water taxi, which is very expensive (€90 or so), but can work out quite well if there are more than a couple of you. The advantage is that you can go directly to your hotel, or very close by. And it's an exciting trip. You can book in the arrivals hall, then pay by cash on board (Ⓐ Consorzio Motoscafi Venezia Ⓣ 041 541 50 84). Otherwise simply go to the landing stage. Only cash is accepted on water taxis.

If you are flying by Ryanair to the tiny airport at Treviso, around 40 km (25 miles) from Venice – which has limited facilities – you will have to get in to Venice itself (45 minutes) or go to Marco Polo airport, by bus or taxi. Check with Ryanair (Ⓦ www.ryanair.com).

By rail

Trains stop at Santa Lucia station, in the Cannaregio area on the Grand Canal. Make sure you don't get off at Venezia Mestre station on the mainland. You will find an information office and places to eat at Santa Lucia. You can get a water bus (Ⓝ No. 1 or 82) down the Grand Canal from there, or a water taxi. Ⓦ www.trenitaliaplus.com

By road
Buses and coaches all stop at the Piazalle Roma, from where you can walk, or take the No. 1 or 82 water bus down the Grand Canal. Cars can get no further either, and there are few places to park (Piazzale Roma, the island of Tronchetto and, on the mainland, in Mestre). Charges are very high. It really isn't advisable to take a car to Venice. Check Ⓦ www.asmvenezia.it and www.veniceparking.it

FINDING YOUR FEET
There are no cars in Venice beyond the Piazzale Roma, so traffic isn't a problem. But by mid-morning, you will find the place overrun by other visitors. So it's best to try to get out early to see the sights, and to avoid the crowds and queuing. Alternatively, go late.

Remember to take care when walking by the sides of canals, or getting on or off water taxis. You should definitely take sensible, comfortable walking shoes, however fashion-conscious you are. And try not to take too much luggage, as you will have to carry it to your accommodation, then back to the station or airport bus. Suitcases with wheels are certainly worth taking.

ⓘ Venice is safe, but you should take sensible precautions against pickpockets, particularly in the many crowds you will come across.

ORIENTATION
San Marco, the Grand Canal, the Rialto, the Accademia Bridge and Santa Maria della Salute are the main landmarks that will guide you

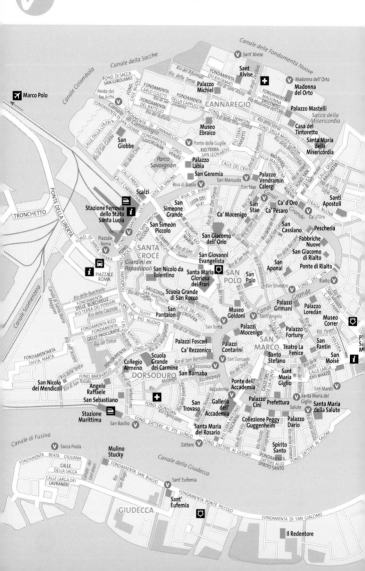

Laguna Veneta

San Michele

Murano
Burano
Torcello

Cimitero
Comunale

Venice

0   250 metres
0   250 yards

N

Canale delle

ISOLA DI
SAN MICHELE

Fondamente
Nuove

Gesuiti

Ⓥ ....Vaporetto Stop
♱ ....Cathedral
ℹ ....Information
🔲 ....Police Station
✈ ....Airport
🚆 ....Railway Stn
🚌 ....Bus Station
✚ ....Hospital

San Lazzaro
ai Mendicanti

Ospedale Civile

Celestia

Scuola di S Marco

Santa Maria
dei Miracoli

Santi Giovanni
e Paolo

San Francesco
della Vigne

CASTELLO

San Lorenzo

Santa Maria Formosa

Scuola di Giorgio
degli Schiavoni

Dársena
Grande

Rio delle Vergini

Fondazione
Querini
Stampalia

San
Giorgio
dei Greci

San
Zaccaria

San Pietro
di Castello

Museo
Diocesano

La Pietà

San Martino

Torri dell'
Arsenale

Piazza
San
Marco

Palazzo
Ducale

Basilica
di San
Marco

San Zaccaria

Arsenale

Museo Stórico Navale

SANT'
ELENA

ISOLA
DI SANT'
ELENA

Bacino di
San Marco

Canale di San Marco

SECCO MARINA

Giardini
Pubblici

Giardini/Biennale

VIALE 24 MAGGIO

San Giorgio

San Giorgio
Maggiore

ISOLA DI
SAN GIORGIO
MAGGIORE

Biennale
d'Arte

Zitelle

Le Zitelle

Teatro
Verde

Lido

around Venice. But it is easy to get lost, as the warren of small canals, bridges and passageways can be very confusing when you try to work out which direction you are going in.

Amazingly for a city that has so many visitors, there are few signs. Those that exist are mostly to San Marco, Rialto, Accademia and the railway station (Ferrovia), but they can also be confusing. If in doubt, head for San Marco. Alternatively, simply follow the crowds, all of which will almost certainly be heading to one of the above. In any case, it is essential to get a detailed map, with a proper street index. If you get lost, don't worry about asking a shopkeeper or waiter in a bar or café for directions. They will usually be helpful.

GETTING AROUND
In Venice, you get around by foot, water or most likely a combination of the two.

Water buses
Water buses (*vaporetti*) are punctual, regular and dependable. (The time of the next water bus is given on electronic displays at bus stations.) You can buy a ticket in advance or pay on board.

DISTRICTS AND STREETS: UNDERSTANDING ADDRESSES
❶ It is important to note that buildings are numbered according to district (*sestiere*), not street. So it can sometimes be difficult to find an address when you only have the district number, and no street name. However, in this guide the street name is given wherever possible. The *sestiere* are: San Marco, Castello, Cannaregio, San Polo, Santa Croce and Dorsudoro.

Water buses zigzag along the Grand Canal and other routes. So they are a good way of crossing the Canal without having to find a suitable bridge. What's more, buses for both directions use the same stops – so make sure you get on a bus going in the direction you want. If you get on a bus going in the wrong direction, simply get off at the next stop and take a bus going to your destination. The fares are flat rate, whether you travel one stop or several. The most useful buses to go up and down the Grand Canal are the No. 1 and No. 82. Going from one end of the Grand Canal to the other takes around 30 minutes. The No. 1 also goes to the Lido, and the No. 82 to Giudecca and San Giorgio.

ⓘ If you are staying in Venice for more than a day and intend to see a lot of sights, it is well worth getting a Venice card. There are various types: for transport, for transport and municipal museum

🔺 *Water taxis are convenient, but expensive*

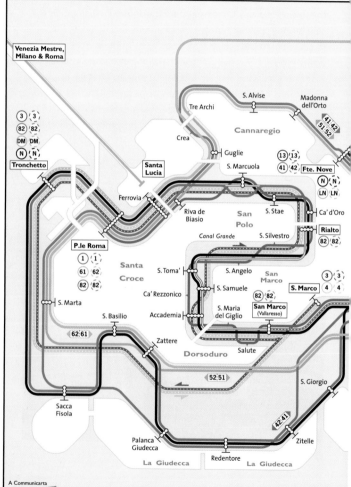

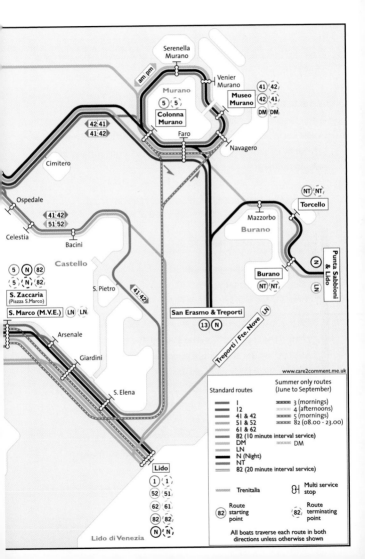

entry, and other services. Check with Ⓦ www.venicecard.com.
The card is available from Vela, ACTV (the water bus company:
Ⓣ 041 271 47 47, freephone 800 40 08 88 Ⓦ www.velaspa.com) and
tourist offices.

Water taxis

Water taxis can be found at various locations (particularly along the
Grand Canal) and can be ordered by your hotel. But they are
extremely expensive, even for short journeys, and journeys need to
be paid for in cash.

❶ Always check the price before you board a water taxi.

IF YOU GET LOST, TRY ...

Excuse me, do you speak English?
Mi scusi, parla inglese?
Mee scoozee, parrla eenglehzeh?

**Excuse me, is this the right way to the old town/the city
centre/the tourist office/the station/the bus station?**
Mi scusi, è questa la strada per città vecchia/al centro
città/l'ufficio informazioni turistiche/alla stazione ferroviaria/
alla stazione degli autobus?
*Mee scoozee, eh kwehstah lah strahda perr lah cheetta
vehkyah/ahl chentraw cheetteh/looffeechaw
eenforrmahtsyawnee tooreesteekeh/ahlla stahtsyawneh
ferrawvyarya/ahlla stahtsyawneh delee ahootawboos?*

▶ *The Doge's Palace – fabulous Venetian Gothic architecture*

San Marco & Castello

St Mark's Square (Piazza San Marco) was described by Napoleon as 'the drawing room of Europe'. It has been the heart of the city for more than a millennium, and today you will mingle with hundreds, or even thousands, of others there.

At the eastern end of the square is St Mark's Basilica. Next to it is the Palazzo Ducale (Doge's Palace). Opposite is the Campanile (bell tower) from which you can get excellent views of the city.

The western end houses the Correr Museum and the Ala Napoleonica (the building joining the two sides of the square). It is the newest part of the square. The north side, the Procuratie Vecchie (originally dating from the 12th century, but rebuilt after a fire in the 16th century) used to be the offices of Venice's powerful magistrates. It also houses the famous Quadri café, dating from 1775.

Just along from Quadri is the Torre dell'Orologio, Venice's heavily embellished Renaissance clock tower. The arch beneath it leads to the Mercerie – Venice's main shopping area. The south side of the square housed the Procuratie Nuove, and was completed in the early 17th century. There you will also find the legendary Caffè Florian, opened in 1720, and once as much a club as a café, attracting great writers and artists. The wood-panelled and mirrored interiors are worth taking a look at in their own right. Both Florian and Quadri have small orchestras. They are both big tourist draws, and – expensive though they are – you shouldn't miss experiencing the atmosphere of San Marco by having a coffee or glass of wine at one of them.

In front of the Doge's Palace is an area called the Piazzetta. There you will see two granite pillars (the columns of San Marco and San Teodoro), topped with winged lions – the symbol of Venice.

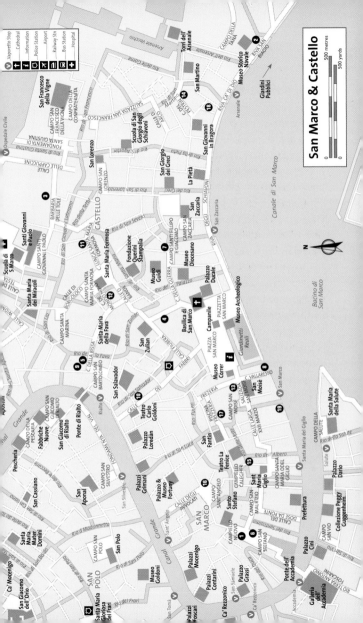

Dating from the 12th century the columns marked the entrance to Venice when you could only arrive at the city by sea. From there you can see the islands of San Giorgio and Giudecca, and the church of Santa Maria Della Salute, just at the beginning of the Grand Canal. The Grand Canal (Canal Grande) winds for about 4 km (2.5 miles) in an 's' shape, and is the city's main artery – with magnificent palazzi and museums along its length.

Around the corner from San Marco, as you turn right from the Piazzetta onto the Grand Canal, you will find the small gardens called Giardinetti Reali ('Royal Gardens') built for Napoleon, and the legendary Harry's Bar.

To the west of San Marco you will find the Palazzo Fortuny, the Palazzo Grassi, the church of Santo Stefano, and the lively square, Campo San Stefano, which houses it. The square has several cafés. Further along is the Accademia Bridge across the Grand Canal, which leads to the Dorsoduro district.

If you head towards the northwest of San Marco (quickest by going to Mercerie and following the signs), you will get to the Rialto Bridge and its colourful, and often very crowded, markets. The Rialto has been a centre of Venetian life for 900 years. The current structure was designed by Antonio del Ponte (his surname, coincidentally, means 'bridge') and was completed in 1591. You will get views of life on the Grand Canal from the top of the bridge, which has small shops (mostly selling souvenirs and tourist items) along it.

If you go east from San Marco, past the side of the Palazzo Ducale, and along the waterfront on the bustling Riva degli Schiavoni, you will be in the *sestiere* (district) of Castello. On your way, you will pass the Hotel Danieli – one of the most famous in Venice. Here, you can get a drink and a marvellous view of the lagoon from the roof terrace.

Apart from the Riva degli Schiavoni, the Castello district isn't one that attracts many visitors. But you will find the major churches of Santa Maria Formosa and Santi Giovanni e Paolo in the area. The latter is next to the city's main hospital (Ospedale Civile). Its astounding marble façade derives from the fact that the building was once home to one of Venice's wealthy philanthropic societies, the *scuole*. The imposing equestrian statue in the square, by Verrochio, is of Bartolomeo Colleoni, the 15th-century mercenary commander. Also in the *sestiere* is the Scuola di San Giorgio degli Schiavoni, which is well worth a visit, and the vast walled Arsenale complex and nearby naval history museum.

The Arsenale, dating from the 12th century, was once the world's greatest shipyard – essential to Venice's naval might. It is largely closed to the public (though you can see its imposing exterior) and is still a naval HQ. During the Biennale, however, some of its buildings are used as exhibition spaces.

If you continue walking along the waterfront beyond the Riva degli Schiavoni, you will reach the *Giardini Pubblici* – the main site of the Biennale, and also one of Venice's few green spaces. It is a tranquil part of the city: shaded and relaxing, with few tourists.

SIGHTS & ATTRACTIONS

Campanile (bell tower)

Made of red brick, and at nearly 100 m (325 feet), this is the tallest building in Venice and one of the city's most prominent landmarks. It was originally built in the 9th century, but took its current shape in 1514. It collapsed in 1902, and a replica was built in 1912. You can take a lift to the top and enjoy great views of the city. That said, try to choose a clear day. Queues can be long.

ⓐ Piazza San Marco ⓒ 09.00–19.00 Apr–June & Sept–Oct;
09.00–21.00 July & Aug; 09.30–16.15 Nov–Mar; last entrance is an
hour before closing time. Admission charge

Palazzo Ducale (Doge's Palace)
Originally constructed in the 9th century as a fortress, but
subsequently destroyed by fire, the present building dates from the
14th and 15th centuries and is in the Venetian Gothic style. It has a
particularly impressive entrance (Porta della Carta), leading to a
courtyard. The palace was the seat of the city's government, and
doges were crowned at the top of the Giant's Staircase (Scala dei
Giganti). Inside, you will find huge and richly decorated chambers,
designed to impress – many with fine paintings by masters such
as Tintoretto and Veronese. Some of the works are massive,
particularly Tintoretto's *Paradise* in the Sala del Maggiore Consiglio
(Hall of the Great Council). You can get from that room to the
Bridge of Sighs (Ponte dei Sospiri), which leads to the prison, which
you can also see.
ⓐ San Marco 1 ⓣ 041 520 90 70 ⓦ www.museicivicveneziani.it
ⓒ 09.00–19.00 Apr–Oct; 09.00–17.00 Nov–Mar. Admission charge

PHOENIX FROM THE FLAMES
To the west of San Marco is the famous 18th-century opera
house of La Fenice. It gets its name ('the Phoenix') from the
fact that it was burned down in 1774. Reopened in 1792, it was
destroyed by fire again in 1836. Unfortunately, the interior was
also heavily damaged by another fire in 1996. It was eventually
restored at the end of 2003 – with new stages, state-of-the art
equipment and a new roof (see page 77).

Palazzo Grassi

This neo-classical palazzo on the Grand Canal was designed by Giorgio Massari in 1749 around a large colonnaded courtyard. It was one of the last palaces built before the fall of the Venetian Republic, and was recently bought by French luxury goods tycoon François Pinault, who got the Japanese architect Tadao Ando to remodel the interior. Pinault has a vast collection of modern art, and – at the time of writing – the plan was that he would display his whole collection, and specially commissioned work, over the next few years, with around 200 works on show at a time. It promises to be an exciting destination for lovers of modern art. It also has a good café. Check the website for exhibition details.

🅐 San Marco 3231, Campo San Samuele 🅣 041 523 16 80

🔵 *The Scuola Grande di San Marco serves as the city hospital's façade*

🌐 www.palazzograssi.it 🕐 10.00–19.00 daily; last entrance is an hour before closing time. Admission charge

San Zaccaria

Originally built in the 9th century, the church is named after St Zacharias, the father of John the Baptist, whose supposed remains are enshrined there in the second altar on the right.

The most noticeable part of the façade dates from the Renaissance (designed by the architect Mauro Codussi, and completed in 1515), but the bell tower was built in the 13th century and the lower part of the façade is Gothic, dating from the late 15th century. The interior is large and dark, a mixture of Gothic and Renaissance styles, though the crypt was part of the 9th century church. The walls of the nave are covered with huge late 17th-century Baroque paintings of variable quality.

The highlight of the church is Giovanni Bellini's *Madonna and Child and Four Saints* (1505), over the second altar on the left. The chapels of St Athanasius and St Tarasius (small admission charge) contain several paintings, including works by Tintoretto (directly in front of you as you enter the first chapel), Van Dyck, Giandomenico Tiepolo, and polyptychs painted by Antonio Vivarini in 1443–4.

📍 Castello 4693, Campo San Zaccaria 🕿 041 522 12 57 🕐 10.00–12.00, 16.00–18.00 Mon–Sat, 16.00–18.00 Sun

Santa Maria Formosa

In one of the liveliest and largest of Venice's squares, this church is not a must-see, but worth popping into. Even if you don't go in, note the grotesque faces on the Baroque bell tower. The present church was designed by Mauro Cadussi in the late 15th century. It has two façades, one on a canal (mid-16th century), and the other in the campo (completed at the beginning of the 17th century). Inside are works by Palma il Vecchio and Bartolomeo Vivarini.

ⓐ Castello 5263, Campo Santa Maria Formosa ❶ 041 275 04 62
ⓦ www.chorusvenezia.org ❶ 10.00–17.00 Mon–Sat.
Small admission charge

Santi Giovanni e Paolo

Also known as San Zanipolo, the church of Saints John and Paul is one of the greatest in the city, in terms of both size and importance. It was consecrated in the early 15th century, and built in the Gothic style for the Dominicans. The doorway, however, is one of the earliest Renaissance designs in Venice, and there are also Renaissance features inside and a Baroque high altar, although the church – built as a Latin cross – is remarkable for its general unity. It was second only to the basilica of San Marco in Venice's public life, which is why you will find fine monuments to no fewer than 25 doges there.

Also worth seeking out is the Chapel of the Rosary (Capella del Rosario), on the far left, for its paintings by Veronese, and the chapel of San Domenico (third on the right) for its ceiling. There is a lovely polyptych (1464) by Giovanni Bellini (second altar on the right).

ⓐ Castello 6363, Campo SS. Giovani e Paolo ❶ 041 523 59 13
❶ 07.30–13.30, 15.30–19.30 daily. Small admission charge

Santo Stefano

Along one side of the lively Campo San Stefano (also known as the Campo Francesco Morosini after the 17th-century doge who lived in the square) is the church of Santo Stefano – worth popping into the fine doorway to see its graceful, and unusual Gothic interior and sumptuous decoration.

Built in the 14th and 15th centuries for the Augustinians, its ceiling is in the shape of ship's keel, and it is decorated in red and white inside. You can also see works by Tintoretto in the sacristy.
ⓐ San Marco 2774, Campo Santo Stefano ⓣ 041 275 04 62
ⓦ www.chorusvenezia.org ⓛ 10.00–17.00 Mon–Sat.
Small admission charge

Basilica di San Marco (St Mark's Basilica)

Once the private chapel of the doges, the church was originally built in the 9th century, but what you will see today mostly dates from the end of the 11th century. Its design was based on a basilica in Constantinople, and Byzantine influences are obvious throughout, including the famous domes and the mosaics inside – over 4,000 sq m (40,000 sq ft) of them. The mosaics on the exterior above the five doors date mostly from the 17th and 18th centuries –

⬤ St Mark's Basilica

with only one 13th-century original (over the north door). The four gilded copper horses, which are one of the symbols of Venice – thought to be Greek or Roman in origin – were part of the plunder brought back from Constantinople in 1204. Those outside are copies, the originals are housed inside the basilica. Built in the shape of a Greek cross, the vast interior contains several chapels, as well as a baptistry, museum and treasury.

ⓐ Piazza San Marco ① 041 522 52 05 ⓛ 09.45–16.30 Mon–Sat, 14.00–16.00 Sun, May–Sept; 09.45–16.30 Mon–Sat, 14.00–16.00 Sun, Oct–Apr. Admission free to main building, but small charges for treasury, museum and other areas

ⓘ Luggage, including backpacks, aren't allowed in the basilica. You have to deposit baggage at Ateneo San Basso (ⓐ Calle San Basso, 315 A).

CULTURE

Museo Correr (Correr Museum) & Museo Archeologico (Archeological Museum)

Entered through the Ala Napoleonica at the western end of St Mark's Square, and housed in the Procuratie Nuove, this museum, celebrating Venice's art and history, is easy to miss but well worth a visit. Although you might want to skip the first rooms, which contain historical artefacts (but also works by Antonio Canova, perhaps Venice's greatest sculptor), you should definitely go to the second floor and wander around the Quaderia picture gallery. There, you will get a very good overview of Venetian art and its development. Look, in particular, for Carpaccio's *Portrait of a Young Man in a Red Hat* and the same painter's *Two Venetian Ladies*. There are also paintings by Jacopo Bellini and his more celebrated sons Giovanni and Gentile.

Your ticket to the Correr Museum also entitles you to visit the Archeological Museum, which is housed in the same complex. It contains Greek, Roman and Babylonian antiquities – particularly sculptures from Greece and Rome, some of which later influenced Venetian artists.

ⓐ Piazza San Marco 52 ⓣ 041 240 52 11
ⓦ www.museicivicivenezizani.it ⓛ 09.00–19.00 Apr–Oct; 09.00–17.00 Nov–Mar; last entrance an hour before closing time. Admission charge.

Museo Fortuny (Fortuny Museum)

Crumbling, but being restored, the 15th-century house (originally the Palazzo Pesaro degli Orfei) of Spanish-born dress and textile designer, painter and photographer Mariano Fortuny is a charming place to visit, though not easy to find. It was left to the city by his widow in 1956. Fortuny's pleated silk dresses were all the rage in the early 20th century. At the time of writing, only one room – covered with Fortuny's famous fabrics and other work – was open. The museum holds regular high quality photographic exhibitions.

ⓐ San Marco 3780, Campo San Beneto ⓣ 041 520 09 95
ⓛ 10.00–18.00 Tues–Sun. Admission charge

Museo Storico Navale (Naval History Museum)

This is a fascinating and well-laid-out museum. On four floors in a former granary near the Arsenale, it features displays showing the history of the Venetian and Italian navies. There are also many other exhibits to do with Venice's relationship with the sea, and maritime life and history in general – including a room devoted to

ⓞ *The hidden treasure of the Fortuny Museum*

L'occhio di Fortuny   Panorami, ritratti e altre visioni

the gondola, and one with a collection of sea shells. It should appeal to many children as well as adults. Note the limited opening times.
ⓐ Castello 2148, Riva San Biagio ① 041 520 02 76 ① 08.45–13.30 Mon–Fri, 08.45–13.00 Sat. Small admission charge

Scuola di San Giorgio degli Schiavoni

The Venetian *scuole*, mainly founded in the 17th century, were charitable societies formed by laymen who had the same background or profession. But many of them became very wealthy, and their impressive buildings house some of the city's finest art works.

The Scuola di San Giorgio degli Schiavoni (also known as Scuola Dalmata dei SS. Giorgio e Trifone), is one of the smallest, but most pleasing to visit. It was founded in the 15th century by Venice's increasingly powerful community of Slavs (Shiavoni). The rectangular ground floor is wood panelled (also notice the impressive wooden ceiling), and contains a cycle of richly coloured and animated paintings by Vittore Carpaccio, depicting the life of St George (the first three on the left) and the other Dalmatian patron saints Tryphon and Jerome – all commissioned in 1502. The staircase, with paintings along it, leads to the upper hall, also wood panelled, with a gilded wooden ceiling further decorated by oval paintings.
ⓐ Castello 3259 A, Calle dei Furlani ① 041 522 88 28 ① 09.30–12.30, 15.30–18.30 Tues–Sat, 15.30–18.30 Sun, Apr–Oct; 10.00–12.30, 15.00–18.00 Tues–Sat, 10.00–12.30 Sun, Nov–Mar. Small admission charge

RETAIL THERAPY

Antichita Marciana A charming shop selling ornaments and velvet fabrics. ⓐ San Marco 1691, Frezzaria ① 041 523 56 66 ① 09.30–13.00, 15.30–19.30 Tues–Sat, 15.30–19.30 Mon

Antiquus One of Venice's best antique shops. ⓐ San Marco 2973, Calle delle Botteghe ❶ 041 520 63 95 ❷ 10.00–12.30, 15.00–19.00 Mon–Sat

Arabe Fenice A leading fashion boutique with exclusive designs. ⓐ San Marco 1822, Frezzaria ❶ 041 522 06 64 ❷ 09.30–13.00, 15.30–19.30 Mon–Sat

Atelier Marega Some of the best masks and carnival costumes (you can rent or buy) in Venice. ⓐ Castello 4968 and 4979, Fondamenta dell'Osmarin ❶ 041 522 30 36

Bevilacqua Near St Mark's Basilica, one of the best places for fine textiles. ⓐ San Marco 337B, Ponte della Canonica ❶ 041 528 75 81 ⓐ 10.00–19.00 Mon–Sat, 09.30–17.00 Sun

Constantini Venetian glass beads, sold as necklaces and bracelets, and also by weight. Note unusual opening hours. ⓐ San Marco 2668 A, Campo San Maurizio ❶ 041 521 07 89 ❷ 15.30–19.30 Mon–Fri, 11.30–18.30 Sat

Ebrû The name comes from a type of marbled paper, and this shop sells some of the finest in Venice. ⓐ San Marco 3471, Campo Santo Stefano ❶ 041 523 88 30 ❷ 10.00–13.30, 14.30–19.00 Mon–Wed; 10.00–13.00, 14.30–19.00 Thur–Sat; 11.00–18.00 Sun

Giovanna Zanella Handmade leather shoes and bags in vivid colours. Not far from the Rialto. ⓐ Castello 5641, Calle Carminati ❶ 041 523 55 00

Il Papiro A good paper shop, where you can buy a range of stationery, and small boxes made of marbled paper. @ San Marco 2764, Calle del Piovan 🕿 041 522 30 55 🕒 10.00–19.30. Also at @ Castello 5275, Calle delle Bande 🕿 041 522 36 48 🕒 10.30–19.00

Il Prato One of the city's more interesting glass shops. @ San Marco 2457, Calle de le Ostreghe 🕿 041 523 11 48 🕒 11.00–19.00 Mon–Sat

Jesuram High quality lace and linen. @ San Marco 4857, Merceria del Capitello 🕿 041 520 61 77 🕒 09.30–19.30 Mon–Sat, 10.30–18.30 Sun

TAKING A BREAK

All' Angelo £ ❶ Sandwiches and snacks, popular with locals. @ San Marco 3464, Campo Santo Stefano 🕿 041 522 07 10 🕒 06.30–23.00 (summer); 06.30–21.00 (winter)

Angiò £ ❷ Along the waterfront not far from St Mark's Square, with delectable snacks and sandwiches (*tremezzini*), and good selection of wine. @ Castello 2142 🕿 041 277 85 55 🕒 07.00–24.00 Wed–Mon (summer); 07.00–21.00 Wed–Mon (winter)

Bandierette £ ❸ Excellent value for lunch (or dinner for that matter). Low key décor, but superior food, enjoyed by many locals. Near the church of Santi Giovanni e Paolo. @ Castello 6671, Barbaria delle Tole 🕿 041 522 06 19 🕒 12.00–14.00, 19.00–22.00, closed Mon evening & Tues

Cavatappi £ ❹ An *enoteca* (wine bar) with tasty snacks during the day, and fuller meals in the evening. @ San Marco 525, Campo della

Guerra ☎ 041 296 02 52 🕐 09.00–24.00, closed Sun evening
& Mon

Gislon £ ❺ Not the most elegant place in town, but good local
dishes at reasonable prices. Near the Rialto. ⓐ San Marco 5424 A,
Calle della Bissa ☎ 041 522 35 69 🕐 09.00–21.30

Le Café £ ❻ A very popular bar and *pasticceria* not far from the
Accademia Bridge. You can get sandwiches, panini, salads, ice cream
and pastries. ⓐ Campo San Stefano 2797 ☎ 041 523 72 01
🕐 08.00–20.30

All' Aciugheta £–££ ❼ A restaurant, bar and café in a tiny square
with several areas both inside and out. You can have a light meal, a
pizza or something more substantial. Or do as many locals do and get
a decent glass of wine and a snack at the modern bar. ⓐ Castello 4357,
Campo Santi Fillipo e Giacomo ☎ 041 522 42 92 🕐 11.00–24.00

Harry's Bar £££ ❽ A full meal here costs an arm and a leg, though
the rich food is surprisingly good for such a famous place, and
served in large portions. No view, unless you sit right next to the
upstairs windows, but pop in downstairs outside dining hours for an
impeccably served sandwich or just one of their famous, but
expensive, cocktails. You never know who you'll see. ⓐ San Marco
1323, Calle Vallaresso ☎ 041 528 57 77 🕐 10.30–23.00

AFTER DARK

Although you can't move for tourists during the day and in the early
evening, the area around San Marco becomes much quieter later on

and is pretty much dead after midnight. Castello is quieter still. But if there is little in the way of late night entertainment, a walk (or *vaporetto* ride) along part of the Grand Canal, or the Riva degli Schiavoni makes up for it. St Mark's Square and the Rialto Bridge, too, take on a new aspect without the crowds.

Restaurants

Alla Botte £–££ ❾ Lively wine bar packed with young people. The restaurant in the back room serves simple, reasonably priced pasta and local dishes. You can also get snacks at the bar. Times given are for hot meals. ❷ San Marco 5482, Campo San Bartolomeo ❶ 041 520 97 75 ⏱ 12.00–15.00, 19.00–22.00 Mon–Wed, Fri & Sat; 12.00–15.00 Sun, closed July

🔺 *Soak up the atmosphere, but sip your drink slowly, at cafés in Piazza San Marco*

A la Campana £–££ ⑩ Good traditional food in a rustic atmosphere. Fine for dinner or lunch – and patronised by many Venetians. ⓐ San Marco 4720, Calle dei Fabbri ⓣ 041 528 51 70 ⓒ 12.00–15.00, 19.00–22.00 Mon–Sat

Alla Mascareta ££ ⑪ A well-known, unpretentious, wine bar with many simple, but tasty offerings. You can stay late. ⓐ Castello 5183, Calle Lunga Santa Maria Formosa ⓣ 041 523 07 44 ⓒ 19.00–02.00, closed Wed & Thur

Alle Testiere ££ ⑫ This small restaurant specialises in fish and seafood subtly flavoured with herbs and spices. Dinner is served in two sittings. ⓐ Castello 5801, Calle del Mondo Novo ⓣ 041 522 72 20 ⓒ 12.00–14.00, 19.00–22.30, Tues–Sat

Bacaro ££ ⑬ A fashionable modern bar and restaurant with prices on the high side, but superior food. You can eat late. Very close to St Mark's square. ⓐ San Marco 1345, Salizada San Moisè ⓣ 041 296 06 87 ⓒ 09.00–02.00

Corte Sconta ££ ⑭ Basic decoration in this well-established restaurant specialising in fish and seafood, which is often packed. There is a small courtyard for hot days. The food is excellent. Try the delicious starter selection (for two), and you probably won't need a main course. ⓐ Castello 3886, Calle del Pestrin ⓣ 041 522 70 24 ⓒ 12.30–14.00, 19.00–21.30 Tues–Sat, closed Jan, mid-July–mid-Aug

Vino Vino ££ ⑮ This wine bar is attached to Antico Martini, one of Venice's oldest restaurants, and has established itself as one of Venice's best – both for food and wine. It is on a small canal. ⓐ San

Marco 2007 A, Calle della Veste ☎ 041 241 76 88 🕐 10.30–22.30,
closed Tues

Acqua Pazza ££–£££ ⑯   A favourite with many, not least because
you can sit out in the square under awnings. The food is mainly
southern Italian, including exemplary pizzas and pasta. But service
can sometimes be offhand, or even rude. ➌ San Marco 3808, Campo
Sant'Angelo 🕐 12.30–14.00, 19.00–21.30 Tues–Sun

Centrale ££–£££ ⑰   Young and trendy, with stylish décor and low
lighting, this 'lounge' is a restaurant and bar, where they serve late.

◓ *Window-shopping in Venice's fashionable Mercerie Street*

Regular live music. ⓐ San Marco 1659 B, Piscina Frezzeria ❶ 041 296 06 64 🕐 18.30–02.00

Al Covo £££ ⓮ One of the best restaurants in Venice, famous for its fish (though good meat also for carnivores) served in comfortable surroundings. Near Riva degli Shiavoni. ⓐ Castello 3968, Campiello della Pescaria ❶ 041 522 38 12 🕐 12.45–15.00, 19.30–22.00, closed Wed & Thur

La Cusina £££ ⓯ The restaurant of the hotel Europa & Regina, and one of the best in Venice – as well as being on the Grand Canal with a view of Santa Maria della Salute. The cooking – based on the freshest local produce, particularly fish – takes account of tradition, but is inventive, with modern presentation. There is a romantic table for two on a small jetty. ⓐ San Marco 2159 ❶ 041 240 00 01 🕐 12.30–14.30, 19.30–22.30

Theatre
The only real entertainment on offer in the area in the evening (apart from the orchestras at Florian and Quadri) is whatever is on at the two theatres.

Teatro Carlo Goldoni The most beautiful theatre in Venice, with performances of Italian classics. ⓐ San Marco 4650 B, Calle Goldoni ❶ 041 240 201 ⓦ www.teatrostabileveneto.it

Teatro La Fenice Venice's famous opera house, risen from the ashes for the third time, with opera, ballet and concert performances. Book well in advance. ⓐ San Marco 1965, Campo San Fantin ❶ Box office: 041 940 200 ⓦ www.teatrolafenice.it

Dorsoduro

Dorsoduro, across the Accademia Bridge, is the area you are most likely to head to after you have seen the sights near San Marco – not least because it is the location of three of Venice's main museums and several fine churches.

The area stretches west to east, with most of its main sights in the eastern part, many of them on the Grand Canal. The far western part is a working class dock area, some of which is being re-developed. The much prettier and more charming east is now full of artists, small galleries and craft shops. Dorsoduro also houses part of Venice's university, so there are many students around.

Just across the wooden bridge from Campo San Stefano in the San Marco area, is the city's main art gallery, the Accademia, containing the finest collection of Venetian art in the world. The Accademia Bridge – only the second to cross the Grand Canal after the Rialto Bridge – was originally built in cast iron in 1854, but was demolished because it was too low. A wooden bridge was erected as a temporary structure in 1932, and was replaced with a replica in 1984. There is a constant stream of people crossing it, but you can get good views of the Grand Canal from there.

A little to the west of the Accademia, on the canal, is Ca' Rezzonico, a palazzo which houses a museum of 18th-century Venice. A short walk to the east of the bridge, and you get to the famous Peggy Guggenheim Museum, with its superb collection of modern art. Beyond the Guggenheim is the magnificent church of Santa Maria della Salute, one of Venice's main landmarks.

At the far eastern end of Dorsoduro is the vast 17th-century Dogana, or customs house. At the time of writing, the plan was to turn this building, with its superb location, into an art gallery. One of

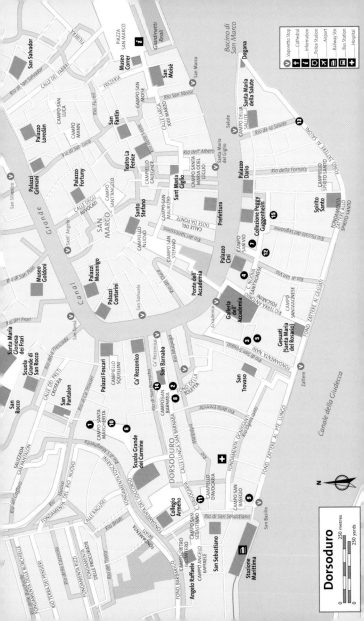

the pleasures of walking along the Grand Canal section of Dorsoduro is to see the magnificent façades of the palazzi and luxury hotels on the San Marco side.

If you go south from the Grand Canal, you will get to the quayside of Zattere, one of the most relaxing and attractive places in Venice to have lunch or a drink. Here you get a view of the island of Giudecca, as well as seeing the local rowing clubs practising. You will also find the church of Santa Maria del Rosario, known as Gesuiti (not to be confused with the more famous church of the same name in Cannaregio).

West along Zattere, the church of San Sebastiano has magnificent interiors painted by Veronese. Nearby, is the Scuola Grande dei Carmini – with its fine Tiepolo ceilings. You will also find both Campo Santa Margherita and Campo San Barnaba in the area. These, particularly the former, are two of Venice's liveliest squares, buzzing with students.

A GONDOLA TO THE GUGGENHEIM

The Guggenheim, located by the Grand Canal, was founded by heiress Peggy Guggenheim (1898–1979), who first opened her collection to the public in 1949 shortly after starting to live in the building that houses the museum. The Guggenheim, although usually packed, offers views of the Canal from the terrace, a pleasant sculpture garden, a bookshop and a good café. But the permanent collection of modern art is what people come for. And, though the museum is relatively small, visitors are rarely disappointed by the quality of art on the walls.
ⓦ www.guggenheim-venice.it/english/index.htm

SIGHTS & ATTRACTIONS

Santa Maria della Salute

Dominating the entrance to the Grand Canal, this domed church, with its gorgeously carved Baroque façade, is an instantly recognised symbol of Venice. *Salute* means 'health', and it was built in thanksgiving for the end of the plague of 1630, when a third of the city's population perished. After a competition, the architect chosen to design it was Baldassare Longhena. Work on the church didn't finish until 1687, five years after Longhena's death. Its importance to Venetians is shown by the fact that, to this day, a pontoon bridge is built from near the Gritti Palace hotel to the church every 21 November for the Festa della Salute.

Given the grandeur of the exterior, the interior – with six side altars – is surprisingly muted, although the marble floor stands out. One of the altars contains Titian's *The Descent of the Holy Spirit* (1550). But the best paintings are to be found in the sacristy, and well worth the small charge. They include Titian's early altarpiece *St Mark enthroned with saints Cosmos, Damian, Roch and Sebastian* (1512) and Tintoretto's *The Wedding at Cana* (1551). ⓐ Campo della Salute ⓣ 041 274 39 11 ⓛ 09.00–12.00, 15.00–18.00 ⓦ www.marcianum.it/salute

San Sebastiano

If you like the sumptuous work of Paolo Veronese (1528–88), this 16th-century church, decorated by him, is the place to go. The painter moved from Verona to Venice as a young man, and lived near the church (where he is also buried). He was commissioned to paint the interior in 1555, and then again in the 1570s. The luminous ceiling paintings depict the life of Esther, and several others show the life of St Sebastian. The unity of the decoration and radiance of Veronese's style make the interior one of the most beautiful in Venice.

ⓐ Dorsoduro 1686, Campo San Sebastiano ⓣ 041 275 04 62
ⓦ www.chorusvenezia.org ⓛ 10.00–17.00 Mon–Sat.
Small admission charge

Gesuati (Santa Maria del Rosario)

If you're walking along the Zattere quayside, it would be a shame not to pay a quick visit to this striking church, designed by Giorgio Massari. Completed 1726–35, it faces Palladio's church of Redentore on the island of Giudecca, and its façade deliberately reflects that of Redentore. Look out inside for the theatrical sculptures by Giovanni Morlaiter and Giambattista Tiepolo's ceiling frescoes.

⬤ Take a stroll over the famous Accademia Bridge

a Dorsoduro 917, Fondamenta della Zattere ai Gesuati **☎** 041 523 06 25 **w** www.chorusvenezia.org **⏱** 10.00–17.00 Mon–Sat. Small admission charge

CULTURE

Galleria dell'Accademia (Accademia Gallery)

This is one of the world's great art galleries, with the finest collection in Venice, situated in three former religious buildings. The collection, started in 1750 as part of an art school, was much enlarged in 1807, when Napoleon gave orders for works confiscated from churches and other religious institutions to be moved there.

The exterior of the museum was being restored at the time of writing, and there are also plans to remodel the interior. This will take some years (probably up to or beyond 2009), so references below are to the layout as it currently exists.

Exhibits are mostly displayed chronologically in 24 rooms, with the earliest Byzantine influenced, and later Gothic devotional works in room 1 (including paintings by Paolo Veneziano).

In rooms 2 and 3 are early Renaissance works by, among others, Giovanni Bellini and Vittore Carpaccio. For most visitors, the highlights of the collection are in rooms 4–11, where you will find some of the greatest art of the high Renaissance, including paintings by masters such as Titian (Tiziano), Tintoretto, Veronese, Giorgione and Mantegna. Look out, in particular for Titian's *St John the Baptist* (1535) and his *Pietà* (his last painting, 1576).

In room 10, Veronese's *Feast in the House of Levi* (1573) is so huge you can't really miss it. It was originally commissioned as a version of the *Last Supper*, but its grand setting and highly-coloured hedonistic content meant that the name had to be altered. All the other canvases in the room are also substantial, including Tintoretto's dark and dramatic *The Translation of the Body of St Mark* (1562), as well as his *The Miracle of the Slave* (1548). Also don't miss Lorenzo Lotto's sensitive *Portrait of a Gentleman* (1525) in room 7, and Giorgione's wonderfully moody and enigmatic *The Tempest* (1507) in room 5.

If you have time, try to visit room 13 (where there are more Tintorettos and work by Jacopo Bassano), rooms 16 and 17 (for 18th-century works by Giambattista Tiepolo and Canaletto) and room 20 for further Renaissance works (including paintings by Carpaccio and Bellini showing Venice in the 16th century).

Room 21 has a marvellous cycle of paintings: *The Life of St Ursula* (1590–5) by Carpaccio. Room 24 has the only work in the building in the place for which it was painted: Titian's outstanding *Presentation of the Virgin* (1538).

ⓐ Dorsoduro 1050, Campo Carita ☎ 041 522 22 47

ⓦ www.artive.arti.benculturali.it ⏰ 08.15–19.15 Tues–Sun, 09.00–14.00 Mon. Admission charge, but free for EU citizens under 19, or over 65

Ca' Rezzonico

If you want to get an idea of the splendour in which the wealthiest Venetians lived, and the interiors of the 18th century, this is the place to come. The Baroque palazzo, designed in 1667 by Baldassare Longhena for the Bon family was unfinished until 1751, when it was sold to the wealthy Rezzonico family. The poet Robert Browning died in the house in 1889, when his son owned it. It has been a museum since 1936.

The palace has several splendid decorative features to admire including massive chandeliers, fine carved furniture, tapestries, ceilings painted by Giambattista Tiepolo and frescoes by

Giandomenico Tiepolo (originally in his own villa). The architectural highlight is the magnificent ballroom, with its gilded wood and *trompe l'oeil* paintings, designed by Giorgio Massari.

In the gallery on the second floor are the only two Canalettos still in Venice, and other 18th-century scenes from Venetian life by Francesco Guardi and Pietro Longhi.

On the third floor is a reconstructed 18th-century pharmacy. Also take time to admire the view from the upper floors.

ⓐ Dorsoduro 3136, Fondamenta Rezzonico ⓣ 041 410 01 00 ⓦ www.museicivicivenziani.it ⓒ 10.00–18.00 Wed–Mon, Apr–Oct; 10.00–17.00 Wed–Mon, Nov–Mar. Admission charge

Guggenheim Museum (Collezione Peggy Guggenheim)

This is one of the most visited museums in Venice. The building itself, with its low Istrian stone façade and pretty garden, is an oddity: actually an unfinished neo-classical palazzo, begun in 1748 – originally designed to be as impressive as others on the Grand Canal.

The Guggenheim is home to Cubist works by Braque, Picasso and Leger among others in the room immediately to the left of the entrance to the collection. A room devoted to surrealist painters such as Magritte, Dali and Max Ernst is on the front left of the building, reached via a corridor containing works by Paul Klee. The rooms on the front right contain paintings by Jackson Pollock and other abstract expressionists.

On the way to the terrace you will see the museum's most recognisable sculpture – of a priapic rider with outstretched arms – Marino Marini's *The Angel of the City*.

ⓐ Dorsorduro 701, Palazzo Venier dei Leoni ⓣ 041 240 54 11 ⓦ www.guggenheim-venice.it ⓒ 10.00–18.00, closed Tues. Admission charge

Scuola Grande dei Carmine

Baldasarre Longhena, also architect of Santa Maria della Salute, was commissioned by the Carmelite order to build this *scuola* (house of a charitable society) next to the church of Santa Maria dei Carmini in 1667. The highlights are Giambattista Tiepolo's nine characteristic ceiling paintings (1740–3) on the first floor. The central panel fell from the ceiling as a result of woodworm in 2000, but has been restored and is now in its old position.

ⓐ Dorsoduro 2617, Campo dei Carmini ❶ 041 528 94 20
🕐 09.00–18.00 Mon–Sat, 09.00–16.00 Sun, Apr–Oct; 09.00–16.00 daily, Nov–Mar. Admission charge

RETAIL THERAPY

Many of the shops near Dorsoduro's main attractions are devoted to arts and crafts. Below are some of the most interesting.

Anniele Embroidered cotton and linen, and some pretty gift items.
ⓐ Dorsoduro 2748, Calle lunga San Barnaba ❶ 041 520 32 77
🕐 09.30–12.30, 16.00–19.30 Mon–Sat

Antichita Lovely antique glass beads, which can be made into necklaces or bracelets for you. ⓐ Dorsoduro 1195, Calle Toletta
❶ 041 522 31 59 🕐 09.30–13.00, 15.30–19.00 Mon–Sat

Fustat Pottery handmade on the premises. ⓐ Dorsoduro 2904, Campo Santa Margherita ❶ 041 523 85 04 🕐 09.30–16.00 Mon–Fri

❶ The Angel of the City, *at the Guggenheim Museum*

Gaulti Imaginative women's accessories, near Ca'Rezzonico.
🅐 Dorsoduro 3111, Rio Tera Canal ☎ 041 520 17 31 🕐 10.00–13.00,
15.00–17.30 Mon–Sat

Il Pavone Near the Guggenheim Museum, very attractive high
quality handmade paper products. 🅐 Dorsoduro 721, Fondamenta
Venier dei Leoni ☎ 041 523 45 17 🕐 09.30–13.30, 14.30–18.30 daily

Madera Contemporary tableware and other design objects.
🅐 Dorsoduro 2762, Campo San Barnaba ☎ 041 522 41 81
🕐 10.30–13.00, 15.30–19.30 Mon–Sat

Mondo Novo Near the Campo Santa Margherita, this is one of the
city's best and most fascinating mask shops, with a huge selection
and a decent range of prices. 🅐 Dorsoduro 3063, Rio Tera Canal
☎ 041 528 73 44 🕐 09.00–18.30 Mon–Sat

Pettenello Unusual toys made by craftsmen. 🅐 Dorsoduro 2978,
Campo Santa Margherita ☎ 041 523 11 67 🕐 09.30–13.00,
15.30–20.00 Mon–Sat

TAKING A BREAK

If you want to relax, go to one of the many cafés along Zattere.
Alternatively, sit on a bench – some of the few in the city – and
picnic. But if you prefer a more vibrant atmosphere, then make your
way to Campo Santa Margherita or Campo San Barnaba; as these
are student hang-outs, prices are fairly reasonable. As always,
remember that bars and cafés near attractions such as the
Accademia will be more expensive than those further away.

Ai Do Draghi £ ❶ A favourite with academics from the
university: good sandwiches, salads, wines, beers, cold meats – and
tables on the square. ⓐ Dorsoduro 3665, Campo Santa Margherita
ⓣ 041 528 97 31 ⓛ 07.30–02.00 (summer); 07.30–22.00 (winter;
not Thur)

Al Artisti £ ❷ A simple stop for a drink or some pasta. Near Campo
San Barnaba. ⓐ Dorsoduro 1196 A, Fondamenta della Toletta
ⓣ 041 523 89 44 ⓛ 08.00–22.00 Mon–Sat

Cantinone gia Schiavi £ ❸ A comprehensive selection of wines
from the Veneto in this bar, and light bites to accompany them.
ⓐ Dorsoduro 992, Ponte San Trovaso ⓣ 041 523 00 34 ⓛ 08.00–20.30
Mon–Sat

Da Gino £ ❹ A bar, popular with students, for very good coffee and
sandwiches. ⓐ Dorsoduro 853 A, Calle Nuova Sant'Agnese
ⓛ 06.00–19.30 Mon–Sat

Gelateria Lo Squero £ ❺ You will find some of the best ice cream
in Venice here. ⓐ Dorsoduro 989, Fondamenta Nani ⓣ 041 241 36 01
ⓛ 10.30–21.00 daily

Orange £ ❻ A cool modern champagne and wine bar, decorated
in orange as the name suggests. Has many student visitors, who
mostly order the Spritz. Good snacks, coffee, cocktails and light
meals, and a view of the square from tables outside. Open late.
ⓐ Dorsoduro 3054, Campo Santa Margherita
ⓣ 041 523 47 40
ⓛ 07.00– 02.00 Mon–Sat, 17.00–24.00 Sun

Vecio Forner £ ❼ A bar, in a small square between the Accademia and the Guggenheim, where you can get excellent coffee, sandwiches, snacks and light hot meals. ⓐ Dorsoduro 671, Campo San Vio ❶ 041 528 04 24 ❷ 08.00–21.00 Mon–Sat

La Bitta ££ ❽ Good for a fuller lunch, from a short seasonal menu, which you can have in the small courtyard in decent weather. ⓐ Dorsoduro 2753 A, Calle Lunga San Barnaba ❶ 041 523 05 31 ❷ 06.30–23.00 Mon–Sat

San Basilio ££ ❾ Serves high quality traditional Venetian cuisine, with a great view of Giudecca. Alternatively, come for drink before lunch or dinner. ⓐ Dorsoduro 1516, Fondamenta Zattere ❶ 041 521 00 28 ❷ 09.30–22.30 Tues–Sat

AFTER DARK

If you want to stay up late, the squares of Santa Margherita and San Barnaba, and the areas immediately around them, are among the few trendy parts of Venice after midnight. A stroll along Zattere is almost as attractive in the evening as it is in the day.

Restaurants

Antico Capon £ ❿ A lively place, where you can sit in the square and enjoy pizzas cooked in a wood oven. ⓐ Dorsoduro 3004 B, Campo Santa Margherita ❶ 041 528 52 92 ❷ 12.00–22.30 Tues–Sat

Avogaria ££ ⓫ The design is chic and modern, but the food is traditional southern Italian from Puglia. The pasta is particularly good, and prices surprisingly reasonable. A light lunch is also good

value. You can sit outside. ⓐ Dorsoduro 1629, Calle d'Avogaria
ⓣ 041 296 04 91 ⓛ 11.30–15.00, 19.30–23.00 Wed–Mon

Cantinone Storico ££ ⓬   Reliable traditional cooking. You can sit
outside, by a canal, in good weather. ⓐ Dorsoduro 660, Calle San
Zuane, Campo San Vio ⓣ 041 523 95 77 ⓛ 12.00–14.00, 19.00–22.00
Mon–Sat

Linea d'Ombra ££ ⓭   Modern décor indoors, but try to get a table
on the terrace for fabulous views of Giudecca and San Giorgio. Very
acceptable food. You can also just go for a drink before lunch or in
the late afternoon. ⓐ Dorsoduro 19, Ponte dell'Umilta
ⓛ 09.00–23.00 Thur–Tues

🔺 *You can't help but admire Santa Maria della Salute*

Oniga ££ ⑭ The female chef is Hungarian, so you will find goulash on the menu in this friendly restaurant. But there are also many Venetian specialities including shellfish and very good pasta dishes. There are tables outside, and it's very good value at lunchtime. ⓐ Dorsoduro 2852, Campo San Barnaba ⓣ 041 522 44 10 ⓛ 12.00–14.30, 19.00–22.30 Wed–Mon

Al Gondolieri £££ ⑮ One of Venice's best and most elegant restaurants with rich, tempting food and wine to match – at a price, but not excessive for the quality of cooking. Near the Guggenheim. ⓐ Dorsoduro 336, Ponte del Formager ⓣ 041 528 63 96 ⓛ 12.00–15.00, 19.00–22.00 Wed–Mon

Bars
Apart from some of the bars mentioned above, others which open late include the following.

Café Blue Rock and blues – both live and recorded – in this student bar. ⓐ Dorsoduro 3778, Calle de la Scuola ⓣ 041 710 227 ⓛ 20.00–02.00 Mon–Fri, 17.00–02.00 Sat & Sun

Il Caffè Attracts students and others with its bustling atmosphere and good wine. Live music on some evenings. ⓐ Dorsudoro 2963, Campo Santa Margherita ⓣ 041 528 79 98 ⓛ 07.00–01.30, Mon–Sat

Round Midnight You can dance at this small bar and disco, which is a student haunt. ⓐ Dorsoduro 3102, Fondamenta dei Pugni ⓣ 041 523 20 56 ⓛ 21.00–02.00 Thur–Sat, closed July & Aug

----

▶ *The Ca' Rezzonico explores 18th-century Venice*

San Polo & Santa Croce

These two adjoining districts, bordered by the northern curve of the Grand Canal, and near both the Piazzale Roma and the railway station, contain the homes of many of Venice's middle class professionals, as well as students. Some of the city's most important sights can also be found in this lively quarter. A word of warning, though: you can easily get lost in the maze of tiny streets, canals and dead ends. If you want to travel by *vaporetto*, the No. 1 will take you to various stops in the area on the Grand Canal.

Along the Grand Canal (not far from the market mentioned in the box below) you'll find Venice's municipal modern art gallery, housed in the magnificent Ca' Pesaro. Then, if you were to see only two more sights in the area, they would have to be Santa Maria

WHAT NEWS FROM THE RIALTO?

The Rialto, an area of high ground, was one of the first settlements (probably as early as the 5th century) in what was to become Venice. It prospered as the mercantile centre of the city from the beginning of the 12th century. The markets of the area (on the San Polo side of the Grand Canal) still thrive. You can take or leave the stalls aimed at tourists (selling trinkets, souvenirs and generally low quality items), but you should have a look at the bustling fish (*pescaria*) and vegetable (*pianta*) markets on the right-hand side as you walk from the Rialto Bridge through the tourist market. Go early to see the produce, landed by barges, displayed at its most colourful and tempting. Stall-holders, particularly in the fish market, tend to start packing up around noon.

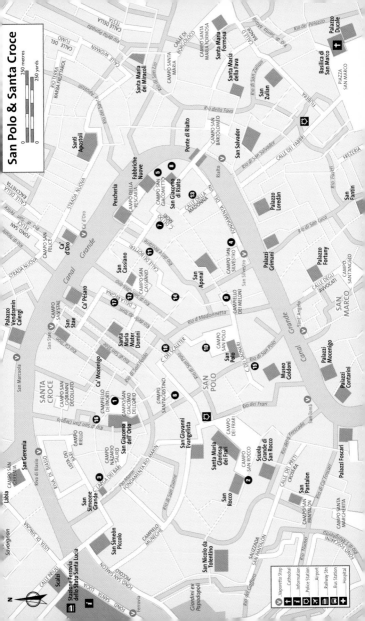

San Polo & Santa Croce

0 250 metres
0 250 yards

N

Palazzo Ducale

Basilica di San Marco

PIAZZA SAN MARCO

Santa Maria Formosa

Santa Maria della Fava

CAMPO SANTA MARIA FORMOSA

San Zulian

Santi Apostoli

Santa Maria dei Miracoli

San Salvador

CAMPO SAN BARTOLOMEO

Ponte di Rialto

Rialto

Pescheria

Fabbriche Nuove

CAMPO DELLA PESCARIA

5
8

CAMPO SAN GIACOMETTO

San Giacomo di Rialto

13

CALLE DELLA MADONNA

7

Palazzo Fortuny

Palazzo Loredan

San Fantin

FREZZERIA

San Cassiano

San Stae

Ca' Pesaro

Palazzo Vendramin Calergi

CAMPO SAN STAE

11
12

Santa Maria Mater Domini

Ca' Mocenigo

4

CAMPO SAN SILVESTRO

Palazzi Grimani

San Aponal

14

CAMPIELLO DEI MELONI

SAN MARCO

CALLE DEGLI AVOCATI

SANT'ANGELO

9

CAMPO SAN POLO

10

SAN POLO

15

Museo Goldoni

Palazzi Mocenigo

Palazzi Contarini

CAMPO SAN GIACOMO DELL'ORIO

1

SANTA CROCE

16

CAMPIELLO DEI MORTI

Ca' Mocenigo

6

CAMPO SANT'AGOSTINO

CAMPO NAZARIO SAURO

San Giacomo dell'Orio

CAMPO RIELLO

San Geremia

San Simeone Grande

3

San Giovanni Evangelista

CAMPO SAN STIN

CAMPO DEI FRARI

Santa Maria Gloriosa dei Frari

2

Scuola Grande di San Rocco

CAMPO SAN ROCCO

San Rocco

San Pantalon

CAMPO SAN PANTALON

Palazzi Foscari

San Simeon Piccolo

Stazione Ferrovia dello Stato Santa Lucia

Scalzi

San Nicolò da Tolentino

CAMPO DEI TOLENTINI

Giardini ex Papadopoli

Vaporetto Stop
Cathedral
Information
Police Station
Railway Stn
Bus Station
Hospital

Gloriosa dei Frari (which contains some of the finest paintings in Venice) and the Scuola Grande di San Rocco, both close to one another.

Also go to the lively Campo San Polo, the second-biggest square in Venice – once a centre for riotous festivities. Take a glance at some of the palaces surrounding the square and pop into its attractive church, if you have time. Alternatively, relax in the quieter Campo San Giacomo dell'Orio. The campo also has an impressive church.

The small but leafy gardens of Giardino Papadopoli, near the Piazzale Roma, offer a haven of calm on a hot or busy day.

SIGHTS & ATTRACTIONS

San Pantalon

This church is technically in Dorsoduro, but is easily reached from the Frari or Scuola Grande di San Rocco. The exterior is mundane, but step inside and be astonished by its remarkable illusionist ceiling – one of the most impressive you will see. The 40 canvases took Gian Antonio Fumiani 24 years to complete, from the start of his commission in 1680.

ⓐ Dorsoduro 3765, Campo San Pantalon ☏ 041 270 24 64
🕒 15.00–18.00 Mon–Sat

San Polo

Spare half an hour to enter the smallish church. Originally built in the Byzantine style in the 9th century, the church was extensively altered in both the 15th century (Gothic style) and in the 19th century (neo-classical). The bell tower dates from the 14th century. The interior is notable for a luminous cycle of paintings by Giandomenico Tiepolo (1727–1804) and a work by his more famous father, Gianbattista. You will also find Tintoretto's *Last Supper* and *Marriage of the Virgin* by Veronese.

ⓐ San Polo 2102, Campo San Polo ☎ 041 275 04 62
ⓦ www.chorusvenezia.org ⏰ 10.00–17.00 Mon–Sat. Small admission charge

Santa Maria Gloriosa dei Frari

Commonly known simply as Frari, the stark brick exterior of this huge Gothic church gives no clue to the splendour of the works of art to be found inside. The current building, in the shape of a Latin cross, dates from the mid-15th century. Its name comes from the fact that the church was built for Franciscan friars. The bell tower is the second tallest in Venice.

Highlights inside include: Titian's stunning *Assumption of the Virgin* (1518), dominating the high altar and his *Madonna di Ca' Pesaro* (1526) in the aisle to the left of the entrance; Giovanni

⬤ *The famous Rialto Bridge*

Bellini's glowing triptych *Madonna Enthroned with Saints* painted in 1488 (sacristy on the far right); and Donatello's wooden statue of *John the Baptist* (1438).

Also look out for the highly decorated rood screen, monuments to the 15th century Doge Foscari and Titian, and the grave of the composer Claudio Monteverdi.

ⓐ San Polo 3072, Campo dei Frari ⓣ 041 275 04 62
ⓦ www.chorusvenezia.org ⓛ 09.00–18.00 Mon–Sat, 13.00–18.00 Sun. Small admission charge

CULTURE

Ca' Pesaro (Galleria Internazionale d'Arte Moderna)

This imposing 17th-century Baroque palace, built for the Pesaro family, was the last project undertaken by Venice's great architect,

⬥ *Stop off at the palatial Ca' Pesaro*

Baldassare Longhena. Work on the façade – one of the most impressive in Venice – was begun in 1673, but Longhena died in 1682, and the building was then completed by Antonio Gaspari in 1703.

Today, it houses two museums: the gallery of modern art, and a section (on the top floors) devoted to oriental art and artefacts. The modern art museum is largely devoted to 19th- and 20th-century Italian painters, but there are also works by Miro, Matisse, Kandinsky, Klimt and Chagall to admire.

The oriental art collection features mainly Japanese arms, armour and other military paraphernalia, as well as paintings, sculpture, musical instruments, pottery and lacquer work.

Don't forget the superb views of the Grand Canal from the upper floors.

🄰 Santa Croce 2076, Fondamenta Ca Pesaro 🄣 041 524 06 62 🄦 www.museiciviciveneziani.it 🄻 10.00–18.00 Tues–Sun, Apr–Oct; 10.00–17.00 Tues–Sun, Nov–Mar; last entrance is an hour before closing time. Admission charge

Scuola Grande di San Rocco

The opulence of the ornate Istrian stone Renaissance façade of this *scuola* indicates the wealth of the charitable brotherhood, which was set up to help the sick. It was named in honour of St Roch (San Rocco), the patron saint of victims of the plague, in the hopes of fending off further pestilence from Venice. The building was completed in 1549. But impressive as the exterior is, it is the interior, painted by Tintoretto over a period of more than 20 years from 1564, that you shouldn't miss. His dark, dramatic, sometimes anguished visions, which cover both walls and ceilings, are simply stunning.

Virtually every one of Tintoretto's 54 paintings of scenes from both the New and the Old Testaments is a masterpiece, but his intensely moving *Crucifixion* (1565) is outstanding. You will find it in the Salla dell'Albergo, next to the main upper hall, and reached by Scarpagnino's grand staircase. Start your visit there, then go to the main hall, and finish your visit in the ground floor hall.

If you can't tire of Tintoretto, you will find more of his work, mostly illustrating the life of St Roch, in the Renaissance church of San Rocco next door.

🅐 San Polo 3052, Campo San Rocco ☏ 041 523 48 64 🕒 09.00–17.30, Apr–Oct; 10.00–16.00 Nov–Mar, closed Easter. Admission charge

RETAIL THERAPY

Aliani A great delicatessen and grocery shop. 🅐 San Polo 654, Ruga Vecchia San Giovanni ☏ 041 522 49 13 🕒 08.00–13.00, 17.00–19.30 Tues–Sat, 08.00–13.00 Mon

Emporio il Nido delle Cicogne Stylish children's clothes. 🅐 San Polo 2806, Campo San Toma ☏ 041 528 74 97 🕒 09.30–12.30, 15.30–19.30 Mon–Sat

Francis Model Leather handbags and briefcases. 🅐 San Polo 773 A, Ruga Rialto ☏ 041 521 28 89 🕒 09.30–19.30 Mon–Sat, 10.30–19.30 Sun

Gilberto Penzo High quality handmade models of gondolas and other boats. 🅐 San Polo 2681, Calle Saoneri ☏ 041 719 372 🕒 10.00–13.00, 16.00–19.30 Mon–Sat

Hibiscus Colourful jewellery and other accessories. 🅐 San Polo 1060, Ruga Rialto ☏ 041 520 89 89 🕒 09.30–19.30 Mon–Sat, 11.00–19.00 Sun

L'Arlecchino A very good carnival mask shop. ⓐ Ruga Vecchia, San Giovanni ⓣ 041 520 82 20 ⓛ 09.30–19.30 Mon–Sat

Polliero Sells fine stationery. You can also get books bound here. ⓐ San Polo 2995, Campo dei Frari ⓣ 041 528 51 30 ⓛ 10.00–13.00, 16.00–19.30 Mon–Sat, 10.00–13.00 Sun

Zazu Chic women's designer shop. ⓐ San Polo 2750, Calle Saoneri ⓣ 041 715 426 ⓛ 10.00–13.00, 15.00–19.30 daily

⬆ *Cross over the Rialto Bridge, then wander to Campo San Paulo*

TAKING A BREAK

Al Prosecco £ ❶ Have a light meal and some wine at this *enoteca*. ⓐ Santa Croce 1503, Campo San Giacomo dell'Orio ⓣ 041 524 02 02 ⓛ 08.00–20.00; later closing in summer

Al Timon £ ❷ A friendly café, designed with a nautical theme, with tempting sandwiches, bruschetta and pasta dishes. Next to the Scuola Grande di San Rocco. ⓐ San Polo 3057 ⓣ 041 713 120 ⓛ 07.00–20.30

Alaska £ ❸ Exciting flavours at this top ice cream stop. ⓐ Santa Croce 1159, Calle Larga dei Bari ⓣ 041 715 211 ⓛ 11.00–24.00 Apr–Oct; 12.00–21.00 Nov–Mar, closed Dec

Altrove £ ❹ Not far from the Rialto Bridge, popular with locals. Have a drink, a salad or a sandwich. ⓐ San Polo 1105, Campo San Silvestro ⓣ 041 528 9224 ⓛ 07.30–01.00 Mon–Sat

Bancogiro £ ❺ Sit outside, on the Grand Canal at the Erbaria, and enjoy a glass of wine, some fresh fish from the nearby market, or a plate of cheese. ⓐ San Polo 122, Campo San Giacometto ⓣ 041 523 20 61 ⓛ 10.30–23.30 Tues–Sun

Da Baffo £ ❻ A lively bar, also selling snacks, favoured by students and academics. Open late. ⓐ San Polo 2346, Campo Sant'Agostino ⓣ 041 520 88 62 ⓛ 07.30–02.00

Do Mori £ ❼ Excellent snacks from the counter. ⓐ San Polo 429, Calle dei Do Mori ⓣ 041 522 54 01 ⓛ 08.00–20.30 Mon–Sat

Naranzaria £ ❽ A restaurant and bar, owned by a count, where you can sit outside and watch life on the Grand Canal. Enter via the Erbaria or Campo San Giacometto. Cold meat, cheese, a few hot dishes and impressive salads. ⓐ San Polo 130, Erbaria ❶ 041 724 10 35 ❶ 11.00–15.00, 18.00–00.30 Tues–Sun

⬤ *The grand façade of the Scuola di San Rocco*

Rizzardini £ 9 One of the best *pasticerria* in the area – selling snacks as well as pastries. **a** San Polo 1415, Campiello dei Meloni **t** 041 522 38 35 **c** 07.00–20.30 Wed–Mon

Birraria £–££ 10 Often full of families in this animated square. Go for the pizza or pasta, or just have a drink. **a** San Polo 2168, Campo San Polo **t** 041 275 05 70 **c** 11.00–23.30

Restaurants

Al Garanghélo £ 11 Friendly place serving hearty food in the evening, and drinks and lighter food – including an array of snacks – during the day. **a** San Polo 1570, Calle dei Botteri **t** 041 721 721 **c** 08.00–22.00 Mon–Sat

Nono Risorto £ 12 Good pizzas as well as Venetian food, which you can eat in the courtyard of this lively place that attracts a young crowd. **a** Santa Croce 2337, Sottoportego de la Siora Bettina **t** 041 524 11 69 **c** 12.00–14.30, 19.00–23.00 Fri–Tues

Alla Madonna ££ 13 Big and crowded (no booking, so you have to queue to get in at busy times), fast service and more than acceptable good-value food. Very near the Rialto Bridge. **a** San Polo 594, Calle della Madonna **t** 041 522 38 24 **c** 12.00–14.30, 19.00–22.00, Thur–Tues

Antiche Carampane ££ 14 Not easy to find, but your search will be rewarded by top-class fish and seafood in this atmospheric trattoria. When weather permits, dine under the stars on the outdoor terrace. **a** San Polo 1911, Calle de la Carampane **t** 041 524 01 65 **c** 12.30–14.30, 19.30–22.30 Tues–Sat

Da Ignazio ££ ⓯ A favourite among local professionals. You can eat traditional Venetian food, impeccably served, in a pretty courtyard. ⓐ San Polo 2749, Calle dei Saoneri ⓣ 041 523 48 52 ⓛ 12.00–15.00, 19.00–22.00 Sun–Fri

Il Refolo ££ ⓰ Pretty views from the outside tables of this upmarket and very fashionable pizzeria (with suitably trendy prices). Also other dishes, and good wines. ⓐ Santa Croce 1459, Campiello del Piovan ⓣ 041 524 00 16 ⓛ 12.00–14.45, 19.00–23.00 Wed–Sun, 19.00–23.00 Tues, closed Nov–Mar

Vecio Fritoin ££ ⓱ High quality ingredients, large portions and a warm welcome in this popular place – with surprisingly good food – offering decent value. ⓐ Santa Croce 2262, Calle della Regina ⓣ 041 522 28 81 ⓛ 12.00–14.30, 19.00–22.30 Tues–Sun

Da Fiore £££ ⓲ Generally considered to be Venice's best restaurant (and not to be confused with a number of other places with similar names). Fish and seafood are the things here. A long, low art deco interior and formal service. ⓐ San Polo 2202 A, Calle del Scaleter ⓣ 041 721 308 ⓛ 12.30–14.30, 19.30–22.30 Tues–Sat

Bars

There isn't much late-night activity in the area, apart from some of the bars mentioned above. That said, you could try the following.

Ai Postali Popular locally, and you can sit outside. You can also eat here. Not far from the train station (across the bridge). ⓐ Santa Croce 821, Fondamenta Rio Marin ⓣ 041 715 156 ⓛ 19.30–02.00 Mon–Sat, closed Aug

Cannaregio

This is the second-biggest of Venice's *sestiere* (districts) after Castello, stretching from the northwest of the city, by the railway station, to near the Rialto Bridge and the main hospital. It has the Grand Canal as its southern boundary and the lagoon to the north.

Cannaregio, which was once Venice's main manufacturing area, has more of a sense of space than other areas. Its broader canal sides and layout make it fairly easy to get your bearings. Apart from many cheap hotels, and the usual tourist shops, it also has the normal everyday shops found in any city. Prices tend to be lower than in other parts of Venice in bars and cafés because most of their clients are locals.

The main route tourists tend to stick to is the Strada Nova (or Nuova) – a broad, hectic street, full of shops and cafés running parallel to the Grand Canal, which leads from near the Rialto Bridge to the magnificent Ca' d'Oro and its museum.

Equally packed with visitors is the Lista di Spagna, near the railway station, full of tourist traps, whether cafés or shops. But venture away from these streets, and you find calm and much evidence of local family life – with washing hanging out to dry from even the grandest-looking buildings, many of them crumbling.

East of the station, and north of the Strada Nova, is the Ghetto area, to which Jews were confined from 1516 onwards. A foundry ('geto') once occupied the area.

The Ghetto, which has given its name to others around the world, was guarded by gates. Jews were allowed out during the day, but only if they wore clothing to identify them. As their numbers grew, they could only build upwards. Napoleon removed the gates in 1797, but the Austrians who subsequently occupied Venice confined the Jews again until the end of their rule.

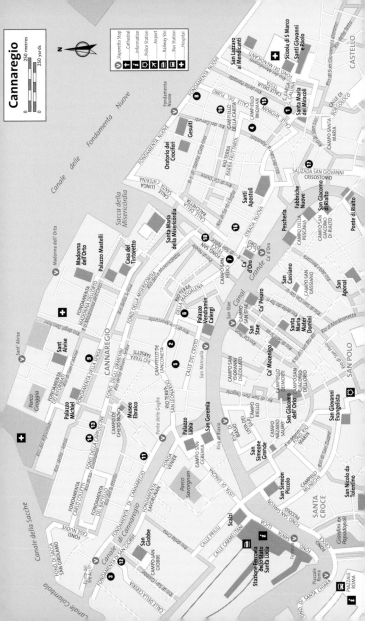

Cannaregio

0   250 metres

0   250 yards

N

Vaporetto Stop
Cathedral
Information
Police Station
Airport
Railway Stn
Bus Station
Hospital

Canale delle Fondamenta Nuove

San Lazzaro al Mendicanti

Scuola di S Marco

Santi Giovanni e Paolo

CASTELLO

Fondamenta Nuove

Gesuiti

Santa Maria dei Miracoli

SALIZADA SAN GIOVANNI CRISOSTOMO

Oratorio dei Crociferi

Sacca della Misericordia

Santi Apostoli

Fabbriche Nuove

San Giacomo di Rialto

Madonna dell'Orto

Madonna dell'Orto

Palazzo Mastelli

Santa Maria della Misericordia

Pescheria

Ponte di Rialto

Casa del Tintoretto

Ca' d'Oro

CAMPO DELLA PESCARIA

Sant'Alvise

Palazzo Vendramin Calergi

San Cassiano

San Aponal

Ca' Pesaro

CAMPO SAN GIACOMO DI RIALTO

SAN POLO

Sant'Alvise

Parco Groggia

San Stae

Santa Maria Mater Domini

CANNAREGIO

Palazzo Michiel

Museo Ebraico

Ca' Mocenigo

San Giovanni Evangelista

Palazzo Labia

San Geremia

CAMPO SAN GIOVANNI DECOLLATO

San Giacomo dell'Orio

San Nicolo da Tolentino

Parco Savorgnan

San Simeone Grande

SANTA CROCE

San Giobbe

CAMPO SAN GIOBBE

San Simeon Piccolo

Scalzi

Stazione-Ferrovia dello Stato Santa Lucia

Giardini ex Papadopoli

PIAZZALE ROMA

Canale di Cannaregio

Although few Jews live there now, there are still a number of Jewish shops and synagogues in the area. There is also the small Museo Ebraico. Just near the Ghetto is the lively Rio Tera di San Leonardo, where you will find a street market in the morning every day except Sunday.

The Fondamenta della Sensa and the parallel Fondamenta della Misericordia to the north of the Ghetto, and near the great church of Madonna dell'Orto, both offer peaceful walks. Tintoretto lived at No. 3399, on the Fondamenta dei Mori near the bridge by the Campo dei Mori. The campo contains statues of three wealthy 12th-century Levantine traders.

From the quayside of Fondamente Nuove, which borders the north of much of Cannaregio, you can get fine views of the lagoon, the cemetery island of San Michele and, beyond it, Murano. At the northern end of the Fondamente is the church of Gesuiti. And between the Fondamente and the Rialto is the lovely church of Santa Maria dei Miracoli.

SIGHTS & ATTRACTIONS

Madonna dell'Orto

This is among the most satisfying churches in Venice to visit. In a small square, it has an attractive, red brick façade with a marble sculpture of St Christopher, to whom it was originally dedicated. The church was founded in the 14th century and modified in the 15th. As a result, the façade is a mixture of Romanesque, Gothic and – in Bartolomeo Bon's doorway – Renaissance styles. Inside, it is pleasantly peaceful, light and uncluttered. But you will find several superb works by Tintoretto, who not only lived around the corner, but is buried there.

ⓐ Campo della Madonna dell'Orto ⓣ 041 275 06 42 ⓦ www.chorusvenezia.org ⓛ 10.00–17.00 Mon–Sat. Small admission charge

Santa Maria dei Miracoli

This small church is much favoured for local weddings. And it would almost certainly win any competition for the most beautiful in Venice – if only for its façade, composed of luminous marble of different colours. Go early in the morning or late afternoon, when it is enhanced by sunlight. Exquisitely designed in Renaissance style by Pietro Lombardo, it was built 1481–9 to house an image of the Virgin by Nicolo di Pietro (now above the high altar), which was thought to be responsible for a number of miracles.

The interior, with some fine sculptures, is almost as lovely, and also uses coloured marble. Also note the 16th-century barrel-vaulted ceiling, with its portraits of saints.

ⓐ Cannaregio 6075, Campiello dei Miracoli ⓣ 041 275 04 62 ⓦ www.chorusvenezia.org ⓛ 10.00–17.00 Mon–Sat. Small admission charge

Gesuiti (Santa Maria Assunta)

The Jesuits built this Baroque church – their first in the city – in the early 18th century. Planned by Domenico Rossi, both the exterior and

---

THE 'REAL' VENICE

Despite its proximity to the station, this is the least visited district of Venice – partly because relatively few of Venice's main sights are to be found there. But it would be a shame not to explore the area, where around a third of the city's population lives, and where you will come closest to finding the 'real' Venice.

interior are strikingly ornate and flamboyant to the point of vulgarity. Don't miss Titian's *Martyrdom of St Lawrence* (1558) above the first altar on the left. And don't confuse the church with the Gesuati in Dorsoduro.

ⓐ Campo dei Gesuiti ❶ 041 528 65 79 ❷ 10.00–12.00, 16.00–18.00

CULTURE

Ca' d'Oro

The façade of 'House of Gold' is one of the most impressive, and best known, of any palazzo on the Grand Canal – perhaps the prime example of Byzantine-influenced 15th-century Venetian Gothic architecture in the city. The building of the palazzo was ordered by the aristocratic merchant Marino Contarini in 1420 and its

⬤ The Ca' d'Oro should not be missed

exterior (originally featuring gold leaf) was designed to be the most luxurious in the city. After a series of subsequent owners, who all made substantial – and sometimes disastrous – alterations to the building, it was restored by Baron Franchetti, and left to the state in 1916.

Franchetti's own collection of art, furniture and tapestries is housed in the museum on two floors. And it is one of the most worthwhile in Venice to spend an hour or so in. The highlight, on the first floor, is Andrea Mantegna's celebrated *St Sebastian* (1506) – worth the entrance charge by itself. Also look out for Carpaccio's early 16th-century *Annunciation* and *Death of the Virgin*.

The entrance is in a small alleyway, off the Strada Nova. You can get good views of the Grand Canal and the Rialto markets from both floors.

ⓐ Cannaregio 3932, Calle della Ca' d'Oro ❶ 041 523 87 90
ⓦ www.cadoro.org ❶ 08.15–19.15 Tues–Sat, 08.15–14.00 Mon; last entrance is 30 minutes before closing time. Admission charge, but free for EU citizens under 19 or over 65

RETAIL THERAPY

Coin Part of a chain, a department store where you can buy clothes and other stylish items at normal prices. ⓐ Cannaregio 5787, Salizada San Giovanni Crisostomo ❶ 041 520 35 81 ❶ 09.30–19.30 Mon–Sat, 11.00–19.30 Sun

Do Maghi At the northern end of the Strada Nova, marvellously colourful glass vases and other objects with modern designs. Also two other branches in town. ⓐ Canneregio 2328 ❶ 041 524 47 19
❶ 09.30–13.00, 14.30–19.00 Mon–Sat, 10.00–19.00 Sun

Gianni Basso A small printing workshop, just off the Strada Nova, where you can order beautiful business cards. 🅰 Cannaregio 5306, Calle del Fumo 🅣 041 523 46 81 🅛 08.30–12.30, 14.00–18.30 Mon–Sat

Gian Paolo Tolotti One of Venice's leading antique shops, with objects to suit most pockets. 🅰 Calle del Forno 42 🅣 041 528 52 62 🅛 09.00–12.00, 16.00–19.00 Mon–Sat

Mori & Bossi The trendiest of shoes. 🅰 Cannaregio 2367, Rio Tera Maddalena 🅣 041 715 261 🅛 09.30–12.30, 3.30–19.30 Mon–Sat

TAKING A BREAK

Da Alberto £ ❶ Good hot and cold food in a comforting environment. 🅰 Cannaregio 5401, Calle Giacinto Gallina 🅣 041 523 81 53 🅛 10.30–15.00, 18.00–22.00 Mon–Sat

Boscolo £ ❷ Get a drink, a slice of pizza or something sweet from this bakery. 🅰 Cannaregio 1818, Campiello de l'Anconeta 🅣 041 720 731 🅛 06.40–20.40 Tues–Sun, closed July, Feb

Canottieri £ ❸ Full of students, and good value for a light lunch or a fuller meal in the evening (mainly fish). 🅰 Cannaregio 690, Fondamenta San Giobbe 🅣 041 717 999 🅛 08.00–15.00, 19.00–23.00 Tues–Sat

Cea £ ❹ Sit outside and get some good value pasta or a salad. Alternatively, just have a drink. 🅰 Cannaregio 5422 A, Campiello Stella 🅣 041 523 74 50 🅛 09.00–22.00 Mon–Fri, closed Sat evening

Do Colonne £ **5** Terrific range of snacks and sandwiches, and the odd hot dish. ⓐ Cannaregio 1814 C, Rio Tera San Leonardo ⓣ 041 524 04 53 ⓛ 10.00–20.30 Sun–Fri

Il Gelatone £ **6** Great flavours in the rich ice cream served here. ⓐ Cannaregio 2063, Rio Terra Maddalena ⓣ 041 720 631 ⓛ 10.30–23.00 May–Sept; 10.30–20.30 Nov–Apr, closed Dec & Jan

▲ *Inside the lovely Madonna dell'Orto are works by Tintoretto*

La Cantina £ **❼** Buzzy bar with excellent snacks. Cannaregio 3689, Campo San Felice ❶ 041 522 82 58 ⏱ 11.00–22.00, Tues–Sat

Algiubagiò £–££ **❽** You can experience inspiring views of the lagoon from the terrace of this restaurant and bar. Have a pizza, a sandwich or something more substantial. ⓐ Cannaregio 5039, Fondamente Nuove ❶ 041 523 60 84 ⏱ 06.30–23.30 Wed–Mon

Anice Stellato £–££ **❾** A local favourite, where you can get reasonably-priced Venetian specialities made from the best ingredients, as well as drinks and snacks (outside dining hours). ⓐ Cannaregio 3272, Fondamenta della Sensa ❶ 041 720 744 ⏱ 10.00–15.00, 18.30–23.00 Tues–Sun

🔺 Strada Nova is the main shopping street in Venice

AFTER DARK

Restaurants

Alla Frasca £ ❿ Pretty *osteria* with southern Italian food and good homemade pasta. ⓐ Cannaregio 5176, Campiello della Carita ⓣ 041 528 54 33 ⓛ 11.00–15.00, 18.30–23.00 Wed–Mon

Fontana £ ⓫ Filled with locals for cheap and cheerful food and atmosphere. You can sit outside. ⓐ Cannaregio 1102, Fondamenta di Cannaregio ⓣ 041 715 077 ⓛ 19.00–22.00 Mon–Sat

Dalla Marisa £–££ ⓬ Rich meat and game dishes are the main thing in this restaurant, which is usually packed – though fish is also on offer. You can sit by the canal in good weather. Make sure that you book. ⓐ Cannaregio 625 B, Fondamenta San Giobbe ⓣ 041 720 211 ⓛ 12.00–14.30, 20.00–21.15, closed Mon, Wed, Thur dinner

Al Bacco ££ ⓭ A friendly traditional place, serving good Venetian food. ⓐ Cannaregio 3054, Fondamenta della Cappuccine ⓣ 041 717 493 ⓛ 07.00–23.00 Tues–Sat, 12.00–15.00 Sun

Bea Vita ££ ⓮ Serving traditional food with a modern twist. Popular with local workers at lunchtime. Big portions. Or go for a drink and some *cichèti* (bar snacks). ⓐ Cannaregio 3082, Fondamenta de la Cappuccine ⓣ 041 275 93 47 ⓛ 09.00–23.00

Boccadoro ££ ⓯ Not easy to find, but worth the effort for great fresh fish and seafood. A few tables outside. ⓐ Cannaregio 5405 A, Campiello Widman ⓣ 041 52110 21 ⓛ 12.30–14.30, 20.00–23.00 Tues–Sat

Ca' d'Oro (Alla Vedova) ££ ⑯ A welcoming place, and a longstanding favourite with locals. Go for a snack during the day or a fuller meal (traditional Venetian) in the evening. ➋ Cannaregio 3912, Ramo Ca' d'Oro ❶ 041 528 55 24 ❶ 11.30–14.30, 18.30–23.30 Fri–Wed, closed Sunday lunch

Fiaschetteria Toscana ££ ⑰ Fine food in a pleasant atmosphere. Mostly, but not entirely, Venetian cuisine. The desserts are particularly famous. ➋ Cannaregio 5719, Salizada San Giovanni Crisostomo ❶ 041 528 52 81 ❶ 12.30–14.30, 19.30–22.30 Thur–Mon, 19.30–22.30 Wed

Vini da Gigio ££ ⑱ A great wine list and very good food, though somewhat leisurely service in this romantic place. Also decent value,

▲ A beautiful, traditional canal house

so it's often full. ❷ Cannaregio 3628 A, Fondamenta San Felice ❶ 041 528 51 40 ❸ 12.00–14.30, 19.30–22.30 Wed–Sun

Bars
Though Cannaregio is pretty quiet at night, there are a few bars open late.

Al Parlamento Not far from the station. Occasional disco music in the evening. Also sandwiches and other food in this bar full of young people. ❷ Cannaregio 511, Fondamenta San Giobbe ❶ 041 244 02 14 ❸ 08.00–02.00

Fiddler's Elbow A popular Irish pub near the Strada Nova. ❷ Cannaregio 3847, Corte dei Pali gia Testori ❶ 041 523 99 30 ❸ 17.00–01.00

Iguana Tex-Mex food and music. ❷ Cannaregio 2515, Fondamenta della Misericordia ❶ 041 713 561 ❸ 18.00–01.00 Tues–Sun

CASINO CHIC
The city's main casino is housed in an early 16th-century Renaissance palazzo, on the Grand Canal. A plaque outside commemorates the fact that Wagner died in the building in 1883. You will need to dress smartly (jacket and tie for men) and be prepared to show your passport.

❷ Palazzo Vendramin Calergi, Cannaregio 2040, Calle Larga Vendramin (off Rio Tera dell Maddalena) ❶ 041 529 71 11 ❾ www.casinovenezia.it ❸ 15.30–02.30 Mon–Thur, 15.30–03.00 Fri, Sat. Admission charge

Tortuga Near the Fondamente Nuove, a pub where you can get snacks during the day. ⓐ Cannaregio 4888, Campo dei Gesuiti ❶ 041 277 01 30 ❷ 10.00–02.00

Paradiso Perduto A restaurant with music, and decent food. A well known and very popular hangout. ⓐ Cannaregio 2540, Fondamenta Misericordia ❶ 041 720 581 ❷ 12.00–02.00 Thur–Sun, 19.00–02.00 Mon

Clubs
Casanova Music Café This is one of the few places in Venice where you can dance. It's an Internet café that turns into a disco at night. Near the train station. ⓐ Cannaregio 158 A, Lista di Spagna ❶ 041 275 01 99 ❷ 23.00–04.00

Theatres
For culture in the evening, the area has two theatres and a cinema.

Giorgione Movie Two screens, mostly showing films dubbed into Italian. ⓐ Cannaregio 4612, Rio Tera dei Francheschi ❶ 041 522 62 98 ⓦ www.comune.venezia.it/cinema

Teatro Fondamenta Nuove Mostly contemporary dance. ⓐ Cannaregio 5013, Fondamente Nuove ❶ 041 522 44 98 ⓦ www.teatrofondamentanuove.it

Teatro Malibran Originally built in 1678, with opera, ballet and classical music. ⓐ Cannaregio 5873, Campiello Malibran ❶ 041 786 601 ⓦ www.lafenice.it

---

❶ *The Lido is Venice's beach resort*

OUT OF TOWN
trips

The Lido, Giudecca & San Giorgio Maggiore

The islands of the southern lagoon are very easy to get to for half a day or more from the city, and well worth it for a change of outlook and atmosphere. There are superb views of Venice from both Giudecca and San Giorgio.

GETTING THERE

To get to the Lido, simply take the No. 1, 51 or 52 *vaporetto*. You can take the No. 1 from anywhere along the Grand Canal, and the Nos. 51 and 52 from the San Zaccaria stop, just along from the Palazzo Ducale. It takes no more than 15 minutes from San Zaccaria. But always check the destination.

The best choice of *vaporetto* to both San Giorgio and Giudecca is the No. 82 from along the Grand Canal or at San Zaccaria. You can also take the No. 82 route across from Zattere, in the Dorsoduro area, near the Gesuiti church. Again, check the destination.

THE LIDO

The Lido, a sandbank 12 km (8 miles) long, is Venice's beach resort, as well as being a residential suburb. With its long, straight roads, broad shaded avenues and cars, it is quite a contrast to Venice itself. It also has mainly modern houses and the villas of the wealthy, several of them in art nouveau or art deco style.

The beach, much of it lined with huts which can be hired, stretches along most of the length of the southern side of the island (a 15-minute walk from the *vaporetto* stop along the main street, the Gran Viale Santa Maria Elisabetta). It is mostly public as well as having areas reserved for the island's hotels.

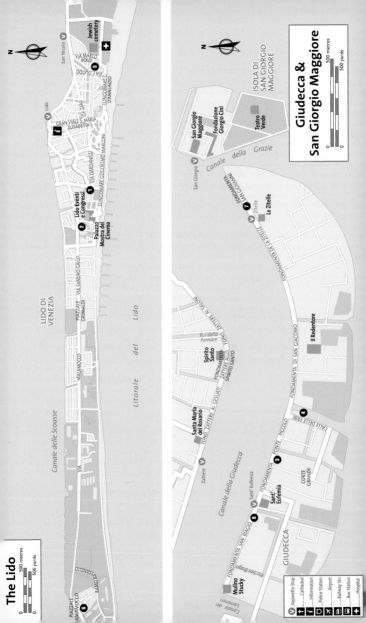

The Lido

0 500 metres
0 500 yards

N

Canale delle Scosse

Canale delle Scasse

LIDO DI VENEZIA

Litorale del Lido

PIAZZALE
ANAFESTO
8

MALAMOCCO

VIA
PIAZZALE VIA SANDRO GALLO
GRIMALDI

Lido

GRAN VIALE S. MARIA ELISABETTA
San Nicolò
i

Lido Eventi
e Congressi
2
Palazzo
Mostra del
Cinema
1
LUNGOMARE GUGLIELMO MARCONI
VIA DARDANELLI

VIA LEPANTO
VIA I MAY
VIA MARCO
POLO
5
VIALE F. DUODO
LUNGOMARE
D'ANNUNZIO
Jewish
cemetery
San Nicolò

Giudecca &
San Giorgio Maggiore

0 500 metres
0 500 yards

N

Canale della Grazie

ISOLA DI
SAN GIORGIO
MAGGIORE

San Giorgio
Maggiore
Fondazione
Giorgio Cini
Teatro
Verde

San Giorgio

Le Zitelle
7
Zitelle
FONDAMENTA DE LE ZITELLE
FONDAMENTA SANT'EUFEMIA / FONDAMENTA S. GIOVANNI

Il Redentore
FONDAMENTA DI SAN GIACOMO

CALLE DELLE ERBE
4

3
FONDAMENTA PONTE PICCOLO
CORTE
GRANDE

Sant'
Eufemia
Sant' Eufemia
8

GIUDECCA

Mulino
Stucky
FONDAMENTA SAN BIAGIO
Rio San Biagio
Canale del
Lavraneri

Canale della Giudecca

Zattere
Santa Maria
del Rosario
FOND. ZATTERE AI GESUATI
Zattere

RIO TERA FORAMANTI
Spirito
Santo
FONDAMENTA
ZATTERE ALLO
SPIRITO SANTO
Rio della
Fornace
ZATTERE AI SALONI

> **Vaporetto Stop**
> + Cathedral
> i Information
> ✈ Airport
> ✕ Police Station
> 🚂 Railway Stn
> 🚌 Bus Station
> + Hospital

To be honest, there aren't any particular sights to see on the Lido. But the village of Malamocco, at the western end of the island where you will find some good fish restaurants, was once the most important settlement in the lagoon, and is the only place on the Lido to have some of the feel of Venice itself. Take bus B from the Gran Viale Santa Maria Elisabetta to get there. The San Nicolò area at the eastern end has a 15th-century fortress, and an 11th-century church – to which the doge was rowed for the festival of La Sensa. It also has a Jewish cemetery dating from 1386.

However, if you want exercise, the Lido is the place for you. Apart from swimming, the Lido offers walks along long roads, cycling, golf and tennis. If you can afford it, have a drink at the Excelsior hotel on the terrace by the beach. And have a look at the Des Bains, where many of the public areas are as they were a century ago.

The main annual event at the Lido is the Venice Film Festival, in late August and early September, when the area around the multi-screen Palazzo Mostra del Cinema and the old casino (where films are also screened) buzzes with activity, and stars hang out at the Excelsior hotel. The festival started at the Excelsior in 1932, and was

A LIDO BIT OF HISTORY

The Lido was developed as a resort in the mid-19th century and became one of the most fashionable in Europe by the beginning of the 20th century – when the luxurious Excelsior and Hotel Des Bains opened. Thomas Mann set much of his novella *Death in Venice* on the Lido, where it was filmed by director Luchino Visconti. The Lido once had a famous casino in a 1930s building of the type associated with Mussolini, but that closed in 2001 and is now used for conferences.

so successful that the Palazzo Mostra del Cinema was built four years later. Its current rather bland and ugly exterior dates from the 1970s.

GIUDECCA

Giudecca was once filled with palaces and pleasure gardens, but by the 19th century had became a site for factories, prisons and store houses. Today, it is a residential suburb of Venice, famous as the location of the Cipriani hotel, one of the most luxurious in the world (see page 35).

The main sight is Palladio's Redentore church – apart, that is, from the views of Venice you can get from the quayside. The western end was being redeveloped at the time of writing, with a Hilton hotel and conference centre being built on the site of the Mulino Stucky, a neo-Gothic flour mill built in 1895, which ceased activity in 1954. If you can make your way to the southern side of the island, you will be rewarded by views of the lagoon.

Il Redentore Finished in 1592, Palladio's magnificent domed church of the Redeemer, by the quayside, was built to give thanks for the end of the plague in the 16th century, which claimed the lives of 50,000 Venetians. A pontoon bridge is laid across the Giudecca canal from Zattere to the church for the Festa del Redentore in late July. Palladio was often inspired by ancient Roman buildings in his plan – in this case the baths of Agrippa. The façade is in a grand classical temple style, but the Capuchin friars who oversaw the building insisted on an interior more modest than it might have been. In the shape of a Latin cross it is, however, as harmonious as any of Palladio's designs. Inside you will find paintings by Vivarini and Veronese – in the sacristy to the right. ❷ Giudecca 195, Campo

del Redentore ☎ 041 275 04 62 ⓦ www.chorusvenezia.org
🕒 10.00–17.00 Mon–Sat. Small admission charge

SAN GIORGIO MAGGIORE

This tiny island, just across the lagoon from St Mark's Square, has two major places of interest: an imposing church and a monastery.

San Giorgio Maggiore One of Venice's key landmarks, the church was planned in 1566 by Andrea Palladio. But the extremely impressive temple façade was only completed in 1611, 31 years after Palladio's death. The interior is capacious, harmonious and beautifully proportioned, adhering to classical principles. You will find two paintings by Tintoretto there – *The Last Supper* and *Manna from Heaven* – and works by Carpaccio and Palma il Giovane. If you go up

● *San Giorgio Maggiore was part of the old Benedictine Monastery*

the recently restored campanile (bell tower), which has a lift, you will get wonderful views of Venice and the lagoon. ⓐ Isola di San Giorgio ⓣ 041 522 78 27 ⓛ 09.30–12.30, 14.30–18.30 May–Sept; 09.30–12.30, 14.30–16.30 Oct–Apr. Small admission charge for campanile

Fondazione Giorgio Cini (Benedictine Monastery) A monastery was first built on the island in the late 10th century, and it soon acquired both considerable wealth and prestige, with many eminent visitors to Venice staying there. One of them, Cosimo de' Medici, commissioned a great library in the 15th century. It was destroyed by fire and replaced by one designed by Baldassare Longhena 200 years later. Andrea Palladio designed the fine refectory and lovely cloisters for the building in the 16th century, when it was enlarged. But the monastery's fortunes changed when Napoleon closed it down. The building later became an artillery headquarters, and was thoroughly neglected. In 1951, however, it was bought by Count Vittorio Cini, in memory of his son, Giorgio. He restored the building and set it up as an international cultural centre. It has also hosted several major international conferences (including the G7 summits in 1980 and 1987). As well as works by Tintoretto, many important temporary art exhibitions are also displayed there. The monastery is also a venue for special events including concerts (check the website for details). ⓐ Isola di San Giorgio ⓣ 041 528 99 00 ⓦ www.cini.it ⓛ Guided tours 10.00–17.00 every 30 minutes Sat & Sun. Admission charge

RETAIL THERAPY

There isn't much in the way of interesting shopping on the Lido, only everyday shops and Italian chain stores on the Gran Viale and

some of the streets near it. Giudecca has very few shops. However, on the Lido, try the following.

Oviesse A moderately-priced department store with a supermarket. ⓐ Via Corfu 1, Lido ① 041 526 57 20 ⓛ 09.00–20.00 Mon–Sat, 09.00–16.00 Sun

TAKING A BREAK

Pasticceria Maggion £ ❶ Excellent pastries. ⓐ Via Dardenelli 46 A, Lido ① 041 526 08 36

Trento £ ❷ This bar serves simple but tasty food, which is very popular with the locals at lunchtime. ⓐ Via Sandro Gallo 82 E, Lido ① 041 526 59 60 ⓛ 07.00–21.00 Mon–Sat

Alla Palanca £–££ ❸ A friendly welcome, reasonable prices and a great view at this bar and restaurant. ⓐ Giudecca 448, Fondamenta del Ponte Piccolo ① 041 528 77 19 ⓛ 07.00–20.30, Mon–Sat

Altanella ££ ❹ A fish restaurant with a terrace. ⓐ Giudecca 268, Calle delle Erbe ① 041 522 77 80 ⓛ Thur–Tues

La Favorita ££ ❺ The Lido's finest restaurant serves Venetian and other dishes in a refined and soothing atmosphere. You can sit outside in summer. ⓐ Via Francesca Duodo 33 ① 041 526 16 26 ⓛ 12.30–14.30, 19.30–22.30 Wed–Sun, 19.30–22.30 Tues

◐ *Il Redentore dominates Giudecca's skyline*

Trattoria Scarso ££ ❻ A simple, traditional fish restaurant in the village of Malamocco on the Lido. ⓐ Piazzale Malamocco 5 ❶ 041 770 834 ❻ Wed–Mon, closed Mon dinner

Cip's Club ££–£££ ❼ The Cipriani has restaurants indoors, on a terrace, and by its pool, but the most fun – with superb views of Venice – is Cip's, where you can sit in the evening on a wooden terrace jutting into the Giudecca canal and enjoy pasta, wood-fired pizza or a more substantial meal. Smart casual dress code.

⬢ *Enjoy a meal with a view at Cip's*

Giudecca 10, Fondamenta de la Zitelle 041 520 77 44

19.30–23.30, closed Jan–Mar

Harry's Dolci ££–£££ An offshoot of Harry's Bar, famous for its sandwiches and pastries (10.30–23.00), but also a very good restaurant, with lower prices than Harry's, and great views from the terrace. Giudecca 773, Fondamenta San Biagio 041 522 48 44 Full meals: 12.00–15.00, 19.00–22.30 Wed–Sun, closed Nov–Mar

ACCOMMODATION

Belvedere ££ Very near the *vaporetto* stop, a straightforward hotel. Piazzale Santa Maria Elisabetta 4, Lido 041 526 60 15 www.belvedere-venezia.com

Villa Cipro ££ A good choice on the northern side of the Lido, with pleasantly decorated rooms and pretty courtyard. Via Zara 2, Lido 041 731 538 www.hotelvillacipro.com

Hotel des Bains ££–£££ Steeped in history and rooms with a sea or garden view. It has a pool and a private beach. Lungomare Marconi 17, Lido 041 526 59 21 www.starwood.com Closed Nov–Apr

Excelsior £££ The most luxurious address on the Lido, this Moorish palace has seen its fair share of celebrities come and go. Everything is top class, including the pool and private beach. There is a regular boat shuttle into Venice. Lungomare Marconi 41, Lido 041 526 02 01 www.starwood.com Closed Nov–Apr

Murano, Torcello & Burano

The ancient lagoon islands of Murano, Torcello and Burano are worth visiting to experience a contrast to the bustle of Venice. Murano is the nearest to Venice itself, and easier to get to, but you will get a feel for life in the lagoon from any of them. The trip across the lagoon is also worth it in itself.

GETTING THERE

The easiest way to get to Murano (other than water taxi) is to take the No. 41 or 42 *vaporetto* from the Fondamente Nuove. It takes much longer to get to Torcello and Burano, and the cheapest way is to take a Linea LN (Laguna Nord) water bus from either San Zaccaria, or (a shorter trip) from the Fondamente Nuove. The LN also stops at Murano. You can also take organised tours to all three islands.

MURANO

Murano is a series of nine small islands linked by bridges. It has been famous for its glass since 1291, when glassmakers were moved there from Venice because of the fear of fires being caused by their furnaces. The glass industry brought wealth, and at one time the island was actually self-governing, with a population of 30,000. Now, only 5,000 people live there.

Today the glass industry still thrives, and Murano glass is exported around the world. Murano itself is a shadow of what it must have been in its heyday, so most visitors go to see the glass shops and demonstrations of glass-blowing in its factories – many of which are closed at the weekend, particularly Sunday. There is also a glass

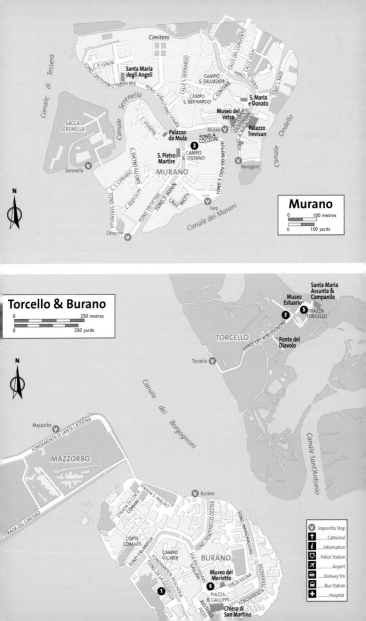

Murano

Cimitero

Canale di Tessera

FOND. C. P. VENINI

Santa Maria degli Angeli

FOND. CRISTOFORO P. PARMENSE

CALLE S. BERNARDO

CALLE DEL CONVENTO

FOND. DEL CONVENTO

CALLE VOLPI

CALLE VIVAI

FOND. SANTI

FOND. NAVAGERO

FOND. D. RADI

CAMPO S. SALVADOR

C. CONTERIE

CAMPO S. BERNARDO

FOND. SEBASTIANO VINER

FOND. SERENELLA

Canale Serenella

S. Maria e Donato

Museo del Vetro

Palazzo Trevisan

FOND. A. COLLEON

FOND. M. GIUSTINIAN

Museo V

SACCA SERENELLA

C. VIVARINI

Palazzo da Mula

Canale di Serenella

FOND. D. BATTURI

Palazzo Trevisan

Serenella V

C. S. CIPRIANO

C. DIETRO GLI ORTI

C. BERTOLINI

S. Pietro Martire

CAMPO S. STEFANO ❸

FOND. GIOV. DEI BATTURI

MURANO

Navagero V

Canale Ondello

FOND. SERENELLA

FOND. DEI VETRAI

FOND. D. MANIN

CALLE RAMOTTI

Faro

Colonna V

Canale dei Marani

N

0 ——— 100 metres
0 ——— 100 yards

Torcello & Burano

0 ——— 250 metres
0 ——— 250 yards

N

Mazzorbo V

FONDAMENTA DI SANTA CATERINA

MAZZORBO

STRADA DEL CIMITERO

Museo Estuario ❷

Santa Maria Assunta & Campanile ❺

PIAZZA TORCELLO

FOND. DEL BORGOGNONI

TORCELLO

Ponte del Diavolo

Torcello V

Canale dei Borgognoni

Canale Sant'Antonio

Burano V

STRADA DI CORTE COMARE

STRADA S. MAURO

CORTE COMARE

FOND. CAVANELLA

FOND. DI LA PESCHERIA

CAMPO VIGNER

FONDAMENTA D. CAO MOLECA

FOND. PONTINELLO DESTRA

VIA S. MARTINO DESTRA

VIA AL GRADO

Museo del Merletto ❹

PIAZZA B. GALUPPI

VIA DI VIGNA

FOND. MAMMACHENO

FONDAMENTA TERRANOVA

BURANO

Chiesa di San Martino

❶

V	Vaporetto Stop
†	Cathedral
i	Information
◉	Police Station
✈	Airport
▣	Railway Stn
▤	Bus Station
✚	Hospital

museum, Murano's old basilica, and the nearby church of San Pietro Martire, which contains two superb works by Giovanni Bellini.

Museo del Vetro Exhibits are arranged chronologically in the 17th-century Palazzo Giustinian, once home of the bishops of Torcello. They range from ancient Roman glass (on the ground floor), to Murano glass dating from the 15th century to the present day – some of it magnificent. ⓐ Fondamenta Giustinian 8, Isola di Murano ⓣ 041 739 586 ⓦ www.museicivicivenezia ni.it ⓛ 10.00–17.00 Apr–Oct, 10.00–16.00 Nov–Mar; last entry 30 minutes before closing, closed Wed

Santi Maria e Donato The basilica, by the Fondamenta Giustinian, is thought to have been founded in the 7th century. The main façade is clearly Byzantine influenced, with a colonnaded apse. The interior of the basilica has a nave and side aisles, and five Greek marble columns down each side. The floor (from 1140) and the apse both feature mosaics. The square bell tower is also characteristic of the 12th- and 13th-century Veneto-Byzantine style, though the conical point is missing from its steeple. The church was restored in the 19th century, but retains its original serenity. ⓐ Campo San Donato ⓣ 041 739 056 ⓛ 09.00–12.00, 15.30–19.00 Mon–Sat, 15.30–19.00 Sun

TORCELLO

Torcello was the first major settlement in the lagoon as people fled the invasions of the mainland in the 5th and 6th centuries. It was also the most important for a time.

It is difficult to believe now, but the marshy island, where only a handful of people currently live, had a population of 20,000 by the

---

▶ *Murano glass is sold all around the world*

14th century, as well as fine palaces and churches. However, it was also unhealthy, and by the 15th century many of its inhabitants avoided the danger of malaria by moving to Venice, which was prospering. From then on, the island was slowly abandoned, and went into decline. Now it is a refreshing contrast to Venice, with a few restaurants and the odd souvenir stall. The main sights are the campanile and the basilica.

Santa Maria Assunta Designed in the Veneto-Byzantine style, the basilica, founded in 639, is the oldest building in the lagoon – though most of what you will see dates from the early 11th century. Look, in particular, at the intricate mosaics on both the floor and walls (the dazzling 'Madonna and Child' in the central apse is a highlight), and the marble rood screen ① 041 270 24 64 ⏰ 10.30–18.00 Mar–Oct; 10.00–17.00 Nov–Feb; last entrance is 30 minutes before closing time. Admission charge

◒ *Visit Murano for its fascinating glass museum*

Campanile A climb to the top of the basilica's bell tower will give you magnificent views of the lagoon. 🕐 10.30–17.30 Mar–Oct; 10.30–17.00 Nov–Feb; last entrance is 30 minutes before closing time in summer, one hour in winter. Admission charge

BURANO

One of the most picturesque places in the whole lagoon, with its vividly coloured houses, the island of Burano has always been noted for its lace-making. The craft, a feature of the island's life since the 15th century, was traditionally undertaken by the wives of local fishermen. It almost died out in the 18th century, and was later revived at the end of the 19th century, but the number of lace makers is dwindling.

There have been fishermen there since the 7th century, and you will see activities associated with fishing throughout this immensely attractive island of 5,000 people – be it nets laid out to

LOOKING FOR LACE?

Burano is famous for its lace, which is why there is a museum dedicated to it. Once the lace-making school, set up in 1871 to help revive the art of lace-making, the **Lace Museum (Museo dei Merletto)** is dedicated to Burano lace, famed for both its delicacy and immense intricacy. There are some superb examples on view – from fans and gloves to tablecloths – some dating from the 16th century. You can also sometimes see lace-makers at work.

ⓐ Piazza Galuppi 187, Isola di Burano ⓣ 041 730 034
ⓦ www.museicivicineveneziani.it 🕐 10.00–17.00 Apr–Oct; 10.00–18.00 Nov–March; last entrance is 30 minutes before closing time. Admission charge

dry, catches being landed or boats being painted and repaired. And, of course – when you've finished looking at the lace shops – the restaurants serve the freshest fish.

The main sight, if you tire of just wandering around, is the lace museum. The Piazza Galuppi, in which the museum is situated, is named after Burano's most famous inhabitant, the 17th-century composer Baldassare Galuppi. The church of San Martino, also in the square, has a tilting bell tower, and a *Crucifixion* by Tiepolo. The square is a good place to relax with a drink.

RETAIL THERAPY

In a nutshell, there is no shopping to talk of on Torcello; but there is glass to buy on Murano and lace on Burano. Make sure what you are buying was actually made locally: many glass and lace shops sell foreign imports. Below are some of the better outlets on Murano and Burano, but there many others.

Barovier & Toso One of the oldest glass makers on Murano, but also impressive contemporary designs. They also have their own museum. Fondamenta Vetrai 28 ⓣ 041 739 049 ⓛ 10.00–12.30, 13.00–17.00 Mon–Fri

Emilia Perhaps the best lace shop on Burano, with lace-making demonstrations from time to time. But not cheap. ⓐ Piazza Baldassare Galuppi 205, Burano ⓣ 041 735 299 ⓛ 09.00–18.30

Luigi Camozzo Specialises in fine engraved glass. ⓐ Fondamenta Venier 3, Murano ⓣ 041 736 875 ⓛ 11.00–13.30, 14.30–18.00 Mon–Fri

Martina A wide range of lace items, including clothing. ⓐ Via San Mauro 307, Burano ⓣ 041 735 523 ⓛ 09.30–18.00

Mazzega Top quality glass. You can also see demonstrations of glass-blowing in the factory on weekdays. ⓐ Fondamenta de Mula 147, Murano ⓣ 041 736 888 ⓛ 09.00–16.00

Rossana e Rossana Traditional Venetian glass, but modern variations, too. ⓐ Riva Lunga 11, Murano ⓣ 041 527 40 76 ⓛ 10.00–18.00

Venini Both new and old designs in this long-established glass-making outlet. ⓐ Fondamenta Vetrai 50, Murano ⓣ 041 273 72 11 ⓛ 09.30–17.30 Mon–Sat

● *Burano has a rather different style to Venice*

TAKING A BREAK

Al Gatto Nero ££ ❶   One of the best and most friendly places in the lagoon, with excellent fresh fish. ⓐ Fondamenta Giudecca 88, Burano ☎ 041 730 120 ⓛ Tues–Sun

Al Trono di Attila ££ ❷   Not far from the basilica. You can eat Venetian food in the pretty garden. Normally lunch only. ⓐ Fondamenta Borgognoni 7 A, Torcello ☎ 041 730 094

Busa Alla Torre ££ ❸   Fish and seafood are naturally the speciality here. Lunch only. ⓐ Campo Santo Stefano 3, Murano ☎ 041 739 662

Da Romano ££ ❹   Traditional lagoon fish and seafood dishes. ⓐ Piazza Galuppi 221, Burano ☎ 041 730 030 ⓛ Closed Tues, Sun dinner

Locanda Cipriani ££–£££ ❺   Run by scions of the Cipriani family, who own Harry's Bar, this restaurant and small hotel (six rooms), is one of the best known places in the lagoon, going since the 1930s. Great authors (including Hemingway, who wrote *Across the River Through the Trees* when staying there), movie stars and other movers and shakers have been attracted here ever since. The restaurant – which spills out onto a charming terrace and garden in the summer – is surprisingly simple, but the food is good, and the service elegant, as you would expect for the prices. You can always just come here for a drink after lunch has been served. ⓐ Piazza Santa Fosca 29, Torcello ☎ 041 730 150 ⓛ 11.00–22.00; closed Mon dinner & Tues

❍ *The Rialto market has served the city for centuries*

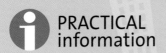

Directory

GETTING THERE

Venice's location in northern Italy makes it easily accessible from anywhere in Europe – or, indeed, the world. Depending on where you begin, the options include air, rail, bus and car, or a combination of these. But arriving in Venice by car is not recommended (except perhaps for a day trip), as you can't drive in the city, and parking is both expensive and limited.

By air

Venice's main airport, Marco Polo, is the third in Italy for air traffic volume. From the UK, you can fly direct by British Airways (Ⓦ www.ba.com), Lufthansa (Ⓦ www.lufthansa.co.uk) and easyJet (Ⓦ www.easyjet.com). Alitalia (Ⓦ www.alitalia.com) has flights via Milan.

Ryanair (Ⓦ www. ryanair.com) flies to Treviso airport, around 40km (25 miles) from Venice (see page 48).

There are no direct flights to Venice from the USA or Canada, but several airlines fly from major US gateways to Milan's Malpensa airport, connected to Venice by direct shuttle or by an easy train connection via Milan's Stazione Centrale (Ⓦ www.trenitalia.it).

From Australia and New Zealand, no direct flights are offered to any Italian city, so the best plan is to book the best price to a major European hub, with an onward connection to Venice itself or Milan.

There are many ready-made packages to Venice. You can also occasionally combine air fare and lodging into a money-saving package on the many travel websites.

Many people are aware that air travel emits CO_2, which contributes to climate change. You may be interested in the possibility of lessening the environmental impact of your flight through the charity Climate Care, which offsets your CO_2 by funding environmental projects around the world.
Visit www.climatecare.org

❶ Especially when booking an entire package, it is wise to secure your trip with travel insurance. Most tour operators offer insurance options, or you can insure the trip independently to protect yourself against surprise cancellations or delays, as well as your luggage and health.

By rail

If you want to travel by land, trains are your best option. A rail trip from London's Waterloo Station to Venice takes just over 17 hours, changing in Paris. If you fly to Milan, and want to take the train to Venice from there, the journey takes around three hours. Trains arrive at Santa Lucia station. Don't get off at Venezia Mestre station, which is on the mainland. Italian trains generally run on time.

❶ Be sure to have your ticket date-stamped in a machine on the platform before boarding
.

RAIL TRAVEL IN STYLE

A luxurious alternative to conventional rail travel is the Orient Express, which has 28 departures from London between April and November. The trip takes 31 hours.
☎ 0845 077 2222 Ⓦ www.orient-express.com

Rail Europe offers a one-stop source of information, reservations and tickets. ⓦ www.raileurope.co.uk

Thomas Cook publishes a monthly European Rail Timetable, giving up-to-date schedules for European international and national train services. ❶ 01733 416477 (UK); 1 800 322 3834 (USA)
ⓦ www.thomascookpublishing.com

Trenitalia ⓦ www.trenitalia.it

⬥ Water buses are reliable and comfortable

By coach

The cheapest way to Venice from the UK – other than a low fare airline booked well in advance – is by coach. The journey takes 25–30 hours from London's Victoria Coach Station.

Eurolines UK ☎ 08705 143219 ⓦ www.eurolines.com

ENTRY FORMALITIES

Visa requirements

UK or Republic of Ireland citizens with a valid passport may stay without a visa for up to 90 days. The same applies to citizens of the USA, Canada, New Zealand and Australia. Citizens of South Africa must have visas to enter Italy.

Customs

EU citizens can bring goods for personal use when arriving from another EU country, but must stick to reasonable quantities for tobacco, wine and spirits. Limits for non-EU nationals are 200 cigarettes (or 50 cigars) and 1 litre of spirits (approx 2 pints) or 2 litres of wine.

MONEY

The euro (€) is the official currency in Italy. €1 = 100 cents. It comes in notes of €5, €10, €20, €50, €100, €200 and €500. Coins are in denominations of €1 and €2, and 1, 2, 5, 10, 20 and 50 cents.

Currency exchange facilities and ATMs are near the arrivals gates at both Marco Polo and Treviso airports. But you are better off using ATMs ('Bancomat'), of which there are many in Venice, as exchange rates at counters are often very poor.

ⓘ Many bars and cafés, small shops and some restaurants do not accept credit and debit cards. So make sure you have enough euros on you, particularly when you arrive. Traveller's cheques are accepted at banks, large hotels and by larger stores, but are difficult to cash elsewhere. You will also have to show your passport. If possible, bring at least one major credit card. Visa and Mastercard are the most commonly accepted.

HEALTH, SAFETY & CRIME

Should you become ill or have an accident, medical care is quite good and free to EU residents who carry a European Health Insurance Card. Non-EU residents should make sure they have travellers' health insurance. Emergency treatment at hospitals is free to everyone. Most good hotels have a list of local doctors on call.

Drinking water is safe in Venice, as is food. However, with so much seafood on offer you can sometimes be unlucky, so it's wise to carry your favourite medication for an upset stomach. Mosquitoes can also be a problem in summer.

ⓘ Pharmacists (recognisable by green or red cross signs) are qualified to give advice about minor ailments. But over-the-counter drugs are more expensive than in Britain or the United States.

While you need to be aware of your surroundings in any city, and avoid walking alone at night and in quieter neighbourhoods, Venice is generally very safe for travellers. However, San Marco, the Rialto and other crowded areas – including the train station and water buses – attract pickpockets. So guard against them by carrying (well

▶ *The police patrol Venice's waterways*

hidden) only the cash you need. Keep cameras firmly in your hand and the strap around your neck. This said, petty theft is not especially common in Venice, and any sort of violence very rare.

There are three types of police: the para-military *carabinieri*, recognisable by the red stripes on their trousers; the *polizia* (state police), and the *vigili* (local police). They can all make arrests. Police officers move around both by foot and boat. You can report a crime to any type of officer, but the paperwork must be completed at a *questura* (police station).

OPENING HOURS

Most major attractions open at 09.00 or 10.00 to 18.00 (sometimes later), with Monday closing. But those in San Marco tend to open earlier, and most attractions have different opening times depending on the season. Smaller ones may have shorter hours, sometimes closing for lunch. Most of the major churches are open 10.00–17.00 in summer.

Most banks open 08.30–13.00 or 13.30 Mon–Fri, and sometimes 14.45–15.45. They are closed on public holidays, and have much shorter hours the day before.

Shops are generally open 09.00 or 10.00 until 19.00 or 19.30 Mon–Sat, sometimes closing for an hour or two at lunch. Some close on Monday. But many shops in tourist areas are open all day, and Sunday opening is also common where tourists abound. Most supermarkets are open 09.00–19.30 Mon–Sat.

Food markets open about 07.00 and close around 12.00–13.00, although the Rialto tourist market (non-food) is open all day. Pharmacies (*farmacia*) are usually open 09.00–13.00 and 16.00–20.00 Mon–Sat, but times vary, and a sign on the door will direct you to the nearest one open, particularly on Sundays and in the evening.

Bars and cafés tend to vary in their hours. Some open early in the morning; others later. Some close at 20.00 or 21.00; others around midnight or even later. However, although snacks may be served throughout the day, hot meals in cafés are usually served at times similar to restaurants: 12.00–14.30 or 15.00, and 19.00–22.00 or 22.30.

ⓘ Many establishments, particularly restaurants, close for a couple of weeks in winter, and/or in July and August. So it's always worth checking and making a booking, particularly at smarter places.

TOILETS

Public buildings, such as museums, usually have clean toilets in the publicly accessible areas near the entrance. But the fastest and easiest solution is to step into a bar or café and have a quick drink there. A much more salubrious alternative is to pop into one of the better hotels for a drink. There are two public toilets near San Marco (one at the Giardini Reali); others at the Rialto, the railway station, at the Piazzale Roma, and in both Cannaregio and Castello. The toilets in Dorsoduro are directly in front of the Accademia Gallery.

ⓘ Public toilets are relatively well signposted and are normally open 08.00–20.00. Be prepared to pay a small fee, usually €0.50.

CHILDREN

Italians love children – and spoil them – but Venice isn't particularly child-friendly, particularly for very young children, because of all the walking, queuing and crossing bridges you will have to do. Some of the smarter restaurants aren't particularly keen on children either, though they will be welcome in simpler cafés and trattorias. On the plus side there are plenty of ice cream and pizza places.

Unfortunately there are also few sights that will appeal to children. But they might enjoy going up the Campanile and visiting the Naval History Museum. Glass-blowing on Murano is fascinating, and travelling by *vaporetto* is fun. Smaller children can play in the Campo San Stefano, or in the Giardini in Castello.

Overall, the Lido, with its beaches, is probably the best place to stay or visit if you have children with you.

❶ Special infant needs, such as baby food and nappies, are available in supermarkets (away from the main tourist areas), but for a shorter stay it is easier to bring familiar brands from home.

COMMUNICATIONS
Phones
All Venice numbers (including the lagoon islands) begin with 041, which must be dialled from inside or outside the city. Note, you still need to dial the 'o' if you are calling from abroad. Apart from the prefix, numbers have either six or seven digits. Numbers beginning with 800 are toll-free.

To make an international call, dial 00, then the country code (UK 44; Republic of Ireland 353; US and Canada 1; Australia 61; New Zealand 64; South Africa 27) and number, omitting the initial zero in UK numbers. To call Venice from outside Italy, dial the international access code (00 in the UK and Ireland; 011 in the US), then Italy's country code of 39, then the number (which will be prefixed with 041 for Venice).

Mobile phone numbers begin with 3. If you see an old number with the prefix 03, omit the zero. UK, New Zealand and Australian mobile phones will work in Italy; US and Canadian cell phones will not.

🛈 To use public telephones, buy a card (*carta telefonica*) from a *tabacchi*, designated by a white T on a dark background. Hotel telephones usually (but not always) carry a high surcharge, so ask at the desk.

Post

Despite what you may have heard, the Italian postal service is quite reliable. For letters and postcards you can buy stamps (*francobolli*) at *tabacchi*. For special services you can go to the main post office at Salizada del Fontego dei Tedeschi, near the Rialto Bridge (🅰 San Marco 5554 🕒 08.30–18.30 Mon–Sat). If you pay extra for *prioritaria*, your card or letter should arrive the next day in Italy, within three days in the UK and about five days elsewhere.

🛈 Rates change often, so check at the *tabacchi* selling the stamps.

Internet

Internet access is increasingly available, both in hotels and at internet points and cafés around the city. Access is rarely cheap at internet cafés, although some offer student discounts. Picture ID is now required to use the internet under Italy's anti-terrorism legislation. Most of the more expensive hotels allow internet access. You can also get internet access at Marco Polo airport. Tourist information offices provide full lists of internet cafés and public access points, but you can try the following.

Casanova Music Café An internet café that turns into a disco late at night. ⓐ Cannaregio 158 A, Lista di Spagna ☏ 041 275 01 99
🕐 Internet: 09.30–23.00

Internet Corner ⓐ Castello 6661 A, Barbaria delle Tole ☏ 041 277 05 15
🕐 10.00–22.00 Mon–Sat

Internet Point ⓐ Dorsoduro 3812 A, Calle dei Preti ☏ 041 714 666
🕐 09.15–20.00

ELECTRICITY

Electrical appliances used in the UK will work in Italy, which runs on 220v, but you will need a two-pin adaptor plug. Those from the US and Canada will need an adaptor, but may also need a transformer to convert from 110v to 220v. It is sensible to buy adaptors before you leave home. Plugs are two- or three-pin, round pin types.

TRAVELLERS WITH DISABILITIES

With its canals, bridges, narrow streets and crowds, Venice is far from the ideal place to visit for those with disabilities. Having said that, the city has taken several helpful steps in recent years. A few bridges now have ramps, several museums have lifts and *vaporetto* stops (and the water buses themselves) should be fairly easy to negotiate – outside the high season, at least, when they can get very crowded.

Disabled travellers wishing to visit Venice should leave home well-informed. Brochures, guides and maps of the city with specific information on accessibility can be consulted and requested from the Informhandicap service of the Venice City Council (ⓐ Viale Garibaldi 155, Mestre ☏ 041 534 17 00 🕐 15.30–18.30 Tues, Thur, Fri; 09.00–13.00 Wed, Sat). The Informahandicap service in Venice itself is at the Public Relations Office (Ufficio Relazioni con il Pubblico) at

ⓐ Ca' Farsetti, S. Marco 4136 ⓣ 041 274 89 45
ⓦ www.comune.venezia.it/handicap
ⓔ informahandicap@comune.venezia.it ⓛ 09.00–13.00 Mon–Sat,
plus 15.00–17.00 Wed

ⓘ To request universal keys, which allow use of the access facilities
installed on four bridges of the San Marco district, you should
contact the above services before departing for Venice. You can also
get help at all APT (local tourist office) information counters (see
Further Information below).

For more details contact the following:

RADAR ⓐ 12 City Forum, 250 City Rd, London EC1V 8AF ⓣ 071 250 3222
ⓦ www.radar.org.uk

SATH (Society for Accessible Travel & Hospitality) advises US-based
travellers with disabilities. ⓐ 347 Fifth Ave, Suite 610, New York,
NY 10016 ⓣ 212 447 7284 ⓦ www.sath.org

FURTHER INFORMATION
Tourist offices
Visit the information counters of the local tourist organisation APT
(*Azienda Promozione Turistica di Venezia*), open every day (excluding
Christmas and New Year). The counters are located at:

Aeroporto Marco Polo ⓣ 041 541 58 87 /529 87 11 ⓛ 09.30–19.30
Piazzale Roma ⓐ ASM (Azienda Servizi Mobilta) Garage ⓣ 041 241 14
99 ⓛ 09.30–13.00, 13.30–16.30
San Marco ⓐ 71 F, Piazza San Marco ⓣ 041 529 87 11 ⓛ 09.00–15.30

San Marco ❷ 2, Giardini Reali ❶ 041 529 87 11 ❹ 10.00–18.00
Stazione Santa Lucia ❷ Railway station ❶ 041 529 87 11
❹ 08.00–18.30
Lido ❸ Gran Viale Maria Elisabetta 6A ❶ 041 526 57 21
❹ 09.00–12.30, 15.30–18.00 June–Oct

The Tourist Office also has its own helpful website at
Ⓦ www.turismovenezia.it

❶ APT offices supply maps, lists of events, accommodation,
guidebooks, information about guided tours and much more
information.

Websites

For *vaporetto* and other bus services Ⓦ www.actv.it
For the city council Ⓦ www.comunevenezia.it
For information about the main churches Ⓦ www.chorusvenezia.org
For information about civic museums
Ⓦ www.museiciviciveneziani.it
For maps, listings and much other information Ⓦ www.ombra.net

❶ *Un Ospite di Venezia* ('A Guest in Venice') is the best publication
for listings, and is available from tourist offices and hotels. You will
also find it on Ⓦ www.aguestinvenice.com

FURTHER READING

Venice has featured in so many books (both fiction and non-fiction)
that it is only possible to give a selective list here.

Non-fiction

The City of Fallen Angels by John Berendt
A History of Venice by John Julius Norwich
My Life by Giacomo Casanova
The Stones of Venice by John Ruskin
Venetian Painting by John Steer
Venice by Jan Morris
Venice for Pleasure by J. G. Links
Venice: The Biography of a City by Christopher Hibbert

Fiction

Acqua Alta by Donna Leon
Dead Lagoon by Michael Dibdin
Death in Venice by Thomas Mann
Don't Look Now by Daphne du Maurier
Eustace and Hilda by L. P. Hartley
Miss Garnett's Angel by Sally Vickers
Othello and *The Merchant of Venice* by William Shakespeare
Serenissima by Erica Jong
The Comfort of Strangers by Ian McEwan
Those Who Walk Away by Patricia Highsmith
The Stone Virgin by Barry Unsworth
The Wings of the Dove by Henry James

Venice plays a large part in the film and TV versions of the life of Casanova, and in the screen adaptations of *The Comfort of Strangers*, *Death in Venice*, *Don't Look Now* and *The Talented Mr Ripley* – as well as many other movies.

Useful phrases

Although English is spoken in many tourist locations in Venice, these words and phrases may come in handy. See also the phrases for specific situations in other parts of this book.

English	Italian	Approx. pronunciation
BASICS		
Yes	Sì	*See*
No	No	*Noh*
Please	Per favore	*Perr fahvawreh*
Thank you	Grazie	*Grahtsyeh*
Hello	Salve	*Sahlveh*
Goodbye	Arrivederci	*Arreevehderrchee*
Excuse me	Scusi	*Skoozee*
Sorry	Scusi	*Skoozee*
That's okay	Va bene	*Vah behneh*
To	A	*Ah*
From	Da	*Dah*
I don't speak Italian	Non parlo italiano	*Nawn parrlaw itahlyahnaw*
Do you speak English?	Parla inglese?	*Parrla eenglehzeh?*
Good morning	Buongiorno	*Booawn geeyawrnaw*
Good afternoon	Buon pomeriggio	*Booawn pawmehreehdjaw*
Good evening	Buonasera	*Booawn sehrah*
Goodnight	Buonanotte	*Booawnah nawtteh*
My name is ...	Mi chiamo ...	*Mee kyahmaw ...*
DAYS & TIMES		
Monday	Lunedì	*Loonehdee*
Tuesday	Martedì	*Marrtehdee*
Wednesday	Mercoledì	*Merrcawlehdee*
Thursday	Giovedì	*Jawvehdee*
Friday	Venerdì	*Venerrdee*
Saturday	Sabato	*Sahbahtaw*
Sunday	Domenica	*Dawmehneeca*
Morning	Mattino	*Mahtteenaw*
Afternoon	Pomeriggio	*Pawmehreedjaw*
Evening	Sera	*Sehra*
Night	Notte	*Notteh*
Yesterday	Ieri	*Yeree*

English	Italian	Approx. pronunciation
Today	Oggi	Odjee
Tomorrow	Domani	Dawmahnee
What time is it?	Che ore sono?	Keh awreh sawnaw?
It is ...	Sono le ...	Sawnaw leh ...
09.00	Nove	Noveh
Midday	Mezzogiorno	Metsawjorrnaw
Midnight	Mezzanotte	Metsanotteh

NUMBERS

One	Uno	Oonaw
Two	Due	Dweh
Three	Tre	Treh
Four	Quattro	Kwahttraw
Five	Cinque	Cheenkweh
Six	Sei	Say
Seven	Sette	Setteh
Eight	Otto	Ottaw
Nine	Nove	Noveh
Ten	Dieci	Dyehchee
Eleven	Undici	Oondeechee
Twelve	Dodici	Dawdeechee
Twenty	Venti	Ventee
Fifty	Cinquanta	Cheenkwahnta
One hundred	Cento	Chentaw

MONEY

I would like to change these traveller's cheques/this currency	Vorrei cambiare questi assegni turistici/questa valuta	Vawrray cahmbyahreh kwestee assenee tooreesteechee/kwesta vahloota
Where is the nearest ATM?	Dov'è il bancomat più vicino?	Dawveh eel bankomaht pyoo veecheenaw?
Do you accept credit cards?	Accettate carte di credito?	Achetahteh kahrrteh dee krehdeehtaw?

SIGNS & NOTICES

Airport	Aeroporto	Ahaerrhawpawrrtaw
Railway station	Stazione ferroviaria	Stahtsyawneh ferravyarya
Platform	Binario	Binahriaw
Smoking/non-smoking	Per fumatori/non fumatori	Perr foomahtawree/non foomahtawree
Toilets	Gabinetti	Gabinetteh
Ladies/Gentlemen	Signore/Signori	Seenyawreh/Seenyawree
Subway	Metropolitana	Metrawpawleetahna

Emergencies

EMERGENCY NUMBERS
Ambulance ⓘ 118
Police (English-speaking helpline) ⓘ 112
Fire Brigade ⓘ 115   **Coastguard** ⓘ 1530

MEDICAL EMERGENCIES
Hospital accident and emergency departments (ask for the *pronto soccorso*) are open 24 hours daily and must treat you free of charge in an emergency. Some doctors speak English.

Venice's main hospital is:
Ospedale Civile ⓐ Castello 6777, Campo Santi Giovanni e Paolo
ⓘ 041 529 41 11; casualty ⓘ 041 529 45 16

On the Lido, the hospital is:
Ospedale al Mare ⓐ Lungomare D'Annunzio 1, Lido ⓘ 041 529 52 34
There are also hospitals on the mainland.

There are pharmacies in all areas of Venice, and you should have no trouble in finding one. Otherwise ask your hotel for the address of the nearest one. You can check *Un Ospite di Venezia* for a list of chemists open in the evening.

POLICE
If you need to report a theft, missing person or any other matter for the police, you can approach a police officer on the street (there are usually several patrolling around St Mark's Square). Alternatively (and preferably) go to a police station. You'll find these at:

ⓐ Castello 4693 A, Campo San Zaccaria ☏ 041 520 47 77
ⓐ Castello 5053, Fondamenta di San Lorenzo ☏ 041 271 55 11
ⓐ Santa Croce 500, Piazzale Roma ☏ 041 271 55 11

CONSULATES & EMBASSIES

Australian Embassy ⓐ Via Antonio Bosio 5, Rome ☏ 06 852 721
ⓦ www.italy.embassy.gov.au
Canadian Embassy ⓐ Via G.B. de Rossi 27, Rome ☏ 06 445 981
ⓦ www.canada.it
Irish Embassy ⓐ Piazza di Campitelli 3, Rome ☏ 06 697 9121
ⓦ www.abasciata-irlanda.it
New Zealand Embassy ⓐ Via Zara 28, Rome ☏ 06 441 7171
ⓦ www.nzembassy.com
South African Consulate ⓐ Santa Croce 466G, Piazzale Roma, Venice
☏ 041 524 15 99 ⓦ www.sudafrica.it
UK British Consulate ⓐ Piazza Donatori di Sangue 2, Mestre
☏ 041 505 59 90
UK British Embassy ⓐ Via XX Settembre 80, Rome ☏ 06 4220 0001
ⓦ www.britishembassy.gov.uk/italy
US Embassy ⓐ Via Veneto 119, Rome ☏ 06 46741
ⓦ www.usembassy.it

EMERGENCY PHRASES

Help! Aiuto! *Ahyootaw!*   **Fire!** Al fuoco! *Ahl fooawcaw!*
Stop! Ferma! *Fairmah!*

Call an ambulance/a doctor/the police/the fire service!
Chiamate un'ambulanza/un medico/la polizia/i pompieri!
Kyahmahteh oon ahmboolahntsa/oon mehdeecaw/la
pawleetsya/ee pompee-ehree!

INDEX

The publishers would like to thank the following for supplying the copyright photos in this book: Pictures Colour Library page 43; all the rest Anwer Bati.

Copy editor: Sandra Stafford
Proofreader: Natasha Reed

Send your thoughts to

books@thomascook.com

- **Found a great bar, club, shop or must-see sight that we don't feature?**

- **Like to tip us off about any information that needs updating?**

- **Want to tell us what you love about this handy little guidebook and more importantly how we can make it even handier?**

Then here's your chance to tell all! Send us ideas, discoveries and recommendations today and then look out for your valuable input in the next edition of this title. As an extra 'thank you' from Thomas Cook Publishing, you'll be automatically entered into our exciting monthly prize draw.

Send an email to the above address (stating the book's title) or write to: CitySpots Project Editor, Thomas Cook Publishing, PO Box 227, The Thomas Cook Business Park, Unit 18, Coningsby Road, Peterborough PE3 8SB, UK.